Also by Richard W. Samson:

The Mind Builder (Dutton)

Thinking Skills (Dutton)

Creative Analysis (Dutton)

The Language Ladder (Dutton)

Problem Solving Improvement (McGraw Hill)

Management by Computer (National Institute of Business Management)

Ask for the Moon -- And Get It (with Percy Ross -- Putnam)

The THINK Program (Innovative Sciences)

MIND

OVER TECHNOLOGY

**Coming Out on Top as a Wired
World Starts to Run on Automatic**

Richard W. Samson

EraNova Institute
New Jersey

Printed and distributed by
Global Book Publisher / BookSurge LLC
A partner of R.R. Bowker
South Carolina

MIND
OVER TECHNOLOGY

First available from Global Book Publisher: January 2004

ISBN: 1-59457-234-8

Print and electronic copies available from --

EraNova Institute: www.eranova.com

BookSurge LLC, a partner of R.R. Bowker:
www.globalbookpeddler.com
5341 Dorchester Road, Suite 16
North Charleston, SC 29418

Barnes & Noble, Amazon.com, and other booksellers in the
U.S. and abroad

Contents

PROBLEM:

1 **What's Going On Here?**
Today's Biggest Trend   9

2 **When Machines Out-muscled Muscle**
Mistakes to Avoid   21

3 **The Electronic Brain Drain**
Big Promise, Big Danger   46

4 **The Technogreed Tsunami**
Undercurrent that's Overwhelming Us   83

SOLUTION:

5 **Becoming Meta-conscious**
Route to Better Jobs & Lives   109

6 **Overcoming Intentional Death**
The Conscious Way to Save Our Skins   137

7 **Restructuring a Self-destructing World**
Making Society Meta-conscious   170

8 **Transforming the Commercial Chameleon**
Restoring the Human Color of Business   191

9 **Mediamorphosis**
*Changing Communications to Support
A Meta-conscious Society*   205

10 **Wealth-creating Opportunities**
Mega-gold in Metamind   222

11 **What You Can Do Now**
Personal Steps for a Better Future   260

THE
PROBLEM

Something's going on that
could be spectacular but spells
trouble and needs fixing.

What is it?

1

What's Going On Here?

Today's Biggest Trend

Today's most significant trend flows beneath the surface of public awareness. Without quite grasping it or putting a name to it, we feel the surge of its promise and the drag of its danger.

What's going on is the biggest transformation in history, one that could thrust us onto lush new shores or plunge us into ugly, black depths. It involves golden and murky blends of mind and technology.

Early Intimations

In my first corporate job after graduating from Whittier College, California, in the early 1960's, I went to work for -- you could guess -- IBM.

They whisked me away from my beautiful, bright new bride, Suzanne, for two weeks of 24/7 indoctrination. With a dozen other cyber-monks, I was to undergo the then-famous "Phase 1."

In a rush of numbers, facts, and machine work, I would learn everything a budding systems engineer should know about the brave new future that would march inexorably to the Internet, artificial intelligence, self-sufficient satellites, automated factories, microchips more plentiful than potato chips, cars getting ready to drive themselves ... cyber-uber-allis. The most significant thing that happened to me during Phase 1 was a dream I had one night.

Fantasy Becomes Reality

In the dream I was lying on my back, bathed in light and surrounded by surgeons in white. With intense focused faces and careful precision, they cut a trap door in my skull and removed about a tablespoon of my brain matter. In its place they slowly, deliberately inserted a metal-and-plastic object. I recognized it as a switching device, one I had been studying earlier that day. The surgeons closed up my head, and all was well. No pain. No apparent after-effects.

The interpretation seemed obvious. Dreams can be metaphors, and they can express groundless fears as well as realities one should heed. New, foreign-seeming but powerful capabilities were being inserted into me. At the same time, maybe I was afraid of losing a bit of my humanity. Looking back at the dream now, I see an expanded interpretation. Back then, I didn't wonder what the surgeons did with the brain tissue they removed. Discarded it, I supposed. What else? Now I wonder, and now I think I know. To explain, I'll add a new scene to the dream:

After discharging me from the operating room, the surgeons don't drop my brain tissue into a slop bucket. They carefully preserve it in a refrigerated container and take it down a long corridor to a large, air-conditioned room. Inside the room, humming eerily, sits a gigantic computer.

They open a hatch exposing the machine's innards and crack the lid of the refrigerated container, releasing a whiff of white condensation. They reach into the container ... and of course implant my brain tissue into the computer's brain. The machine brightens, humming with a bit more intelligence.

From Mind into Electronics

What's happening in the world today is a vast process of "mental transplantation." Into us, and out of us. Thanks to electronic advances, great new capabilities are being incorporated into our minds, our jobs, and lives; but at the same time, our mental processes -- from memory to decision making -- are being rapidly transferred into computers, microchips, networks, and mechanical devices of all types. It's happening in a way that's altering jobs, transferring wealth, and changing lives. Current impacts include --

- **Offshoring of professional and service jobs** (a shift made possible by information technology).

11

- **Automation of more and more tasks,** moving us toward a world that will run on automatic.
- **Conversion of our minds into media dumps** -- passive repositories of consumer information.

Just as our muscle power was transferred into machinery during the rise of the industrial era, today -- as the information age matures -- our *mental* power is being transferred into our tools. This can be a very good thing, but dangers lurk.

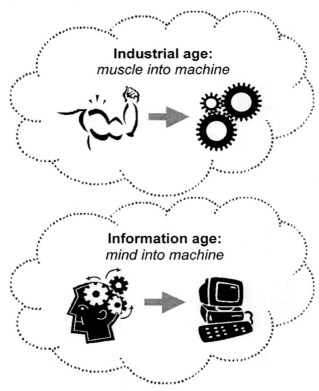

Industrial age:
muscle into machine

Information age:
mind into machine

We should be scared. Exhilarated and giddy, perhaps, but also scared.

Think of the process, in its current predominantly outgoing mode, as a great global brain drain, one that is currently draining dollars as well as mentality. It's the most critically pivotal -- either empowering or suicidal -- trend of our times. Yet while aspects of the trend have made economic and lifestyle headlines, the trend itself is under-reported by the media and remains virtually invisible to the public eye. It has not yet been recognized as the all-pervasive, all-consuming behemoth that it is, and it's not on policy makers' radar screens. Ordinary people, legislators, and corporate leaders scarcely know what's happening let alone what to do about it.

Industrial Age Precedent

Caught up in the almost daily advances in hardware and software (all incorporating memory, decision making, and other capabilities patterned after human mentality) we should be wary of history repeating itself.

Back at the dawning of the industrial age, people who hoped to avoid sweatshops and a diminished quality of life adjusted by moving from labor-intensive jobs to specialized know-how jobs. That won't work during the present transition, because specialized know-how tasks are the very kind being usurped. If we are to avoid being permanently displaced and diminished in

13

favor of smart chips and code (and their manipulators), we need a new strategy for the new transition.

Big Impact on Employment

We can't count on yesterday's jobs for tomorrow's income. During the rise of the industrial age, farm employment never came back, until now it accounts for less than 2% of the U.S. workforce.

Today, thanks to the brain drain of human skills into electronic systems, even the most high-tech jobs are being downsized and restructured rapidly. They'll never resize and some will disappear entirely.

Through corporate "offshoring," millions of technical and service jobs are going to low-paid professionals overseas; but that's only temporary -- the first wave of the change. In time the foreign contractors will also lose out, to all-electronic solutions. No matter how little pay Indians or Pakistanis are willing to accept, no one can work as cheaply as a chip.

Electronic intelligence is now performing much of the mental work formerly done by secretaries and middle managers, accountants and governmental administrators, product designers and corporate planners, soldiers and salespeople, farmers and restaurateurs, stockbrokers and bank tellers, doctors and diplomats, drivers of delivery vans and drivers of industry. Pieces of human mentality have been sucked out of virtually

14

all of us and spewed into networks and chip-enabled devices. "All of us" includes, of course, the mafia, commercial predators, digital pranksters, Al-Qaeda operatives, and nuts dreaming up the next domestic mayhem. To a large extent the human-to-electronic mental transfer is a fait accompli. Many of the things you and I used to figure out, organize, or remember are now being figured out, organized, and remembered by silicon-based systems.

Big Impact on Our Lives

More than our occupations are affected. The mentality we're transferring into electronics has the power to come back at us -- assaulting our minds as consumers and citizens. Formerly dumb media systems have gotten smart; now they're feeding our minds more deftly, with personalization and interactivity. It has happened almost overnight and continues to happen with shocking speed. The outcome could be wonderful or catastrophic. Already the process accounts for much of today's anxiety and feelings of being overwhelmed, assaulted, and manipulated.

We are being enabled and empowered as never before; simultaneously, many of us are also being marginalized and threatened as never before. In addition, companies, social structures, and national economies are being dismantled and restructured at a furious pace. Everything is getting buffeted, changed around, and transformed.

Positive Prospects?

To save us on the job front, will small, new businesses come to the rescue, as in the past? Don't count on it, not for new specialized know-how jobs.

In the past, innovation has always created new forms of employment to replace those lost, and that *can* happen now. But what exactly are those new jobs this time? No one knows. We need to create a whole new kind of work, beyond specialized know-how; and we can. Call it "meta-mental" or "hyper-human" work, described later in this book.

Hyper-human work -- based on metamind skills that are described in chapter 5 -- will gradually become tomorrow's norm (with planning and luck). This brave new work will be based on attributes and abilities that computers are not likely to co-opt -- at least for the next few decades.

In our personal, social, and cultural lives, we need to counter the negative mentality that is making life overly chaotic and prone to aberrations such as over-eating, drug addiction, crime, and terrorism. Through a focus on our most human qualities marshaled by metamind, we can do it, creating a world that works for everyone.

A Great, Gushing Mental Outflow

We're not only going out of our minds but could be losing the fully-empowered use of our minds -- which could lead to loss of our livelihoods, degradation of our lifestyles, and eventually even the end of our existence. But it doesn't have to be that way. The transplantation of mental functions from us to our electronic tools can be an enormously good thing. Our minds, through adept use of electronics, can be amplified with new capability to remember, track, research, and create -- so long as more than a select few control the tools. We can gain unprecedented power to make things happen, create better lives for ourselves, and shape the world we want. However, if we fail to recognize the dark, disempowering side of megatech, we will find that many of our mental services will become unnecessary, and we'll be sidelined.

Sucked Into the Global Brain

Our mental skills and processes are fast flowing not only into our PC's, handhelds, and appliances, but also into the ever-smartening electronic nervous system of our planet, the global brain. Invasive as it already is, the process has only just begun. Infrastructure now in place or in development provides a massive catapult for rapid acceleration of the transference.

Listen to the sucking sound getting louder. It's the sound of your mind being extracted into the electronic cortex with its fibers and wireless pulses extending everywhere. It's happening slurp by tiny slurp:

- **Slurp** ... spell checking done by PC's.
- **Slurp** ... banking and grocery checking done by automated stations.

17

- **Slurp ...** highway tolls collected by electronic pulses bouncing off tags in windshields.

The electronic brain drain with its giant sucking sound is perhaps only five or ten percent complete. There's much more to come. The emerging planetary intelligence will contain great gobs of our smarts. We'll all be connected, but it's unclear just how.

Depending on how the process proceeds and how we adjust, the end result can be incredibly beneficial or just plain awful. The global brain can extend and empower our individual minds in spectacular new ways, or leave us mentally destitute and irrelevant.

For years the mind-into-electronics trend has been gathering silent momentum. We can no longer ignore it. Facile systems are muscling in on our mental work and every facet of our lives.

One way or another the world is going to run on automatic, with us in control or subordinated and silenced. Metamind will make the difference. If we can muster it, we'll be the bright masters of the universe; if not, darker forces will rule.

How This Book Can Help

This book offers an arsenal of cautions and options for better negotiating the perils and prospects ahead. You'll learn --

- Industrial-age mistakes to avoid now.
- Key e-trend dangers to look out for.
- Ways to build wealth in business ventures big and small.
- Ways to keep your mind from becoming an e-media dumping ground.
- How interactivity can be used to manipulate you, and how to avoid it.
- A simple way to raise your consciousness instantly, on the job and off.
- How to help create a mind-based vs. e-dominated society.
- Strategies for sound career choice and advancement.
- How to assert your human edge in daily activities.

You'll also become privy to speculations on possible new "meta" modes of art, science, religion, and culture -- supported by smart electronic systems. And you'll explore the potential for "common consciousness," with and without e-support.

If you're a professional helping to build information-age infrastructure (physical, political, business, educational, community, or cultural) the book offers many action options for your consideration:

- New profit-making ventures and business improvements based on metamind.
- New industrial policies and laws that can ease occupational transition.
- New ways to think about the content and delivery of movies, sitcoms, and sermons.
- New mindsets for creating ads and media that promote good things better than ever.
- New curricula fostering meta-consciousness in our schools and universities (building on the recent popularity of "thinking skills").
- An expansion of the online arsenal of mind-extending tools (a positive complement to company-management software when combined with people-friendly employment policies).
- People-empowering changes to the physical environment, such as the morphing of industrial-age cities and towns into "intercommunities" (described in chapter 7).
- And much more.

Over all, the book will help you join others in charting a path around social chaos and a bleak future, toward a golden age of mind-powered human interaction.

2

When Machines Out-muscled Muscle

Mistakes to Avoid

Today we enjoy history's highest standard of living thanks to technology, but getting here was far from pain-free.

Depressing Experience

My parents got married at the worst of times: the depth of the Great Depression when 16 million people, fully one third of the U.S. workforce, couldn't find jobs.

Unemployment, economists say, serves a useful purpose. It pressures the system to self-correct, leading to eventual economic upturn. Some people just have to suffer; there's no way around it, they say.

My father contributed to the upturn that began at the end of the down decade. He was one of the grunts who took the brunt. Out of work, he headed a dirt-poor household, deep in debt. One of the 16 million, his statistical presence helped motivate Franklin Roosevelt to introduce the New Deal to get the country back on its feet. After Pearl Harbor, my father finally found work in the defense plants that sprang to life on the southern California coast. He never made much and did not thrive in the mass-production culture. Later he left the plants for a series of jobs out in the open -- everything from carpenter to salesman -- with frequent periods of unemployment or illusive contingency pay.

Looking Back

My conclusion is that my father suffered from bad luck in a system that rewarded many but forced some to suffer; and that he was not well-suited to the opportunities and requirements of the industrial era. He might have thrived in the toil and sweat of the agricultural age, or in the multi-faceted interplay of today's dawning information age. But not then.

Though my father mixed like water with the oil of industrialism, he never stopped trying. And he never gave in to the personal or social destructiveness that many in his situation resorted to: alcohol, nicotine, violence, crime, or suicide. He did steal some money out of desperation, but only once; and he paid for it. He died in his 50's of bleeding ulcers, probably caused by stress and worry.

He wasn't a talker like my mother, but one thing he said to me stands out in my memory. We were outside on the grass in front of our broken-down two-story rented house in the middle of an orange orchard. It was a beautiful, sunny day with cawing crows and a few white, drifting clouds in a clear blue sky.

He was dressed in his work shirt and overalls, which he wore when he walked down California Avenue to Whittier Boulevard to catch a bus to the defense plant. Smiling, a rare departure from his chronic worried expression, he playfully jingled some change in his pocket. I was eight or nine years old. I was glad for his smile because I, like most well-treated children, was happy most of the time.

He told me that one day I would have lots of change in my pocket, and lots of folding money, too -- more, much more than I needed. He couldn't give me money. He couldn't give me the skills or knowledge for making money. But he could give me the promise of money, the dream of someday having it.

The last time I saw him I was 14. He was lying limply, pathetically on a hospital bed in Los Angeles. He looked at me with what I think he knew to be his last communication with me. What he gave me was a complex expression that contained the hint of a smile. It was a combination of regret, submission, apology, shame, and hope. The hope was not for himself but for me. Outside of the hospital, I stood with my mother on a strip of concrete waiting to cross the busy L.A. street, so we could find our parked car and go home.

What I remember is the road noise, the relentless movement of the traffic, the absence of trees and grass, and the glaring harshness of reflected sunlight amid blockish buildings. Mostly I remember the noise -- the roar of spinning tires, the hiss of displaced air, the occasional impatient honk of a horn or squeal of brakes -- and the relentlessness of the moving vehicles.

Any one of the cars or trucks could kill you if you stepped in front of it. They kept coming -- unforgiving and inevitable -- and would not stop.

The Past is Prologue

Today we're moving into a transition that's bigger than the Great Depression. It's as big as the entire genesis and progress of industrialism with all its machinery, systems, economics, and social consequences -- which included the Depression as a single stage.

We don't need to re-experience anything like the Depression, or any fender scrapes or bruises beyond those that can't possibly be avoided. We can make sure people have the income they need to support their families, and the chance to make a contribution and live the lives they want.

Lets start by reviewing yesterday's great transition, the childhood and coming-of-age of industrialism. With knowledge of what went wrong then, we can minimize tomorrow's pain and maximize its potential.

Lessons from Yesterday

Technology with its new tools is supposed to make life better, but often makes it worse. That happened when the industrial age engulfed the agricultural age. Consider the changes wrought by technology in agriculture itself. For a farmer trying to eke out a living, easing along on a John Deere was better than slogging behind an ox-drawn plow. It was magic. He could just step on the gas and release the power of a dozen farmhands with oxen. Think of the farmhands, though. For them it wasn't so magic. While field labor may not have been all pleasure, it was familiar and close to home, and also accomplished in pleasant natural surroundings.

It will put an end to back-breaking labor!

Yes ... and the family farm.

25

To the farm boss, the new technology -- tractor or meat grinder -- meant greater ease and reduction of labor costs. To farm hands it meant displacement and often a reduced quality of life. The hands adjusted by leaving their rural homes to toil in factory sweatshops and live in cheap city flats. Eventually, with the help of reformers, their sorry state improved -- if not for them personally, for their sons and daughters.

In every nook of industrial development, we can find examples of the benefits of amplified muscle power; we can also find examples of the pain of muscle replacement.

In the clothing industry --

- Thanks to sewing machines and methods of mass-production, a few women in a dress factory could supply more dresses more cheaply than dozens of seamstresses working at home. It was good for the clothing makers and women who could afford store-bought garments, but ...
- Seamstresses either lost their livelihood or had to abandon their homes for factories.

In the printing and publishing industries --

- Printing presses -- especially automated, power-driven ones -- could churn out thousands of sheets while scriveners scratched away to copy a single page. It was good for publishers and readers and those who found better jobs as typesetters and pressmen, but ...

- Retiring their pens, scriveners had to find other ways to scratch out a living.

In the lumber and home-building industries --

- A lumberjack with a power saw could fell a dozen trees while an axe-man hacked away at just one. Sawmills could spew out countless beams and boards while a carpenter with an adze labored to shape a single piece. It was good for owners, for ordinary people who now could buy quantities of lumber instead of painstakingly shaping their own boards from logs, and for laborers who found better jobs in the mills, but ...
- Old time woodsmen lost their traditional income, and over time people in general started losing the ability to build their own homes as specialism, the hallmark of industry, replaced general know-how and the can-do spirit with narrower sets of machine-related skills.

A better future always seems to exact suffering as the price of entry. Technology extends human capability, but also displaces it -- often in distressing ways. However good the end result, there is a trauma of change. On the plus side, the transition period also offers advancement opportunities for those astute enough to seize them.

Once the transition to the new technology is mature, the trauma of change has usually abated; and the advancement opportunities have been snapped up. We are left with the end results of the mature transition. These, hopefully, are mostly good; but there always seem to be unanticipated negative consequences.

It is vital to bear these realities in mind as we move deeper into the information age, a time when the human mind is becoming dramatically extended and many of us face disconcerting replacement or restructuring of our functions and lives, a time of new opportunity and change-related trauma, a time when a bright future beckons but dire consequences loom.

First let's look a bit more at the transition to the industrial age, the time when our muscle power was extended and displaced.

TRANSITION TO THE INDUSTRIAL AGE
Muscle power was amplified

Transition period	End result
Growth opportunity: People had the chance to develop industrial skills and exploit mass-production technology.	**Positive outcome:** Today we have more abundant food, new products and services and higher standards of living.
Trauma of change: Farmers, craft workers, and others were displaced; lifestyles were disrupted; laborers lost income, had to move, and often ended up in sweatshops while seeking to adjust.	**Negative consequences:** Today food is processed and often less than fresh; we lack exercise, tend to be obese; we suffer from pollution, suburban sprawl, crime and expanding terrorism.

Thanks to machines invented in the 17th through the 20th centuries, our physical power was greatly multiplied. Did it happen in the best possible way and with the best possible results? Did the trauma of change have to be as bad as it was? What negative consequences might have been avoided? What missed growth opportunities might have been seized?

The Pain of Muscle Replacement

While industrial-age technology -- the steam engine, electric motor, automobile -- manufactured a brighter future, many people got chewed up in the gears of change. Too often the promised "better times" pertained to others later, not to them at the time.

Consider the young women who toiled in the Triangle Shirtwaist Factory in New York City a century ago. Their often-reported plight offers historical insight and moral lessons. A fire there, on March 25, 1911, brought America's deplorable sweatshop condition to public notice.

One hundred and forty six died; more than 50 of these threw themselves from windows and ledges, choosing death by impact over death by suffocation and barbecue. Aghast onlookers saw them fall and heard them thud and splash. The fire may have been an accident, but the conditions that permitted the tragedy were not. There were no sprinkler systems; there was inadequate fireproofing; there were no safety standards. Furthermore, the women had no way to get out of the work area; they were routinely locked in so union organizers could not get at them.

While industrialism brought new, more affordable goods and services, it scorched people on the production end of things. Workers lost their full spectrum of humanity when viewed through the green lenses of economic eyeglasses. They became, to early capitalists, like machines -- expendable units of production, components of cost that had to be minimized and could be abused.

QUESTION:

How many workers died in the course of building Hoover Dam?
- None
- 3
- 17
- 96
- Nobody bothered to keep good count.

Nobody knows how many workers died while laboring on Hoover Dam, whose cascading waters would power countless laborsaving machines and appliances. Accurate records were not kept. Estimates range from 96 to 112 based mostly on newspaper reports.

Three men died in an explosion as a tunnel was being driven into the canyon wall 150 feet above the Colorado River. Another was crushed between two trucks. Another died of a fractured skull when struck by a power shovel. There are stories that several men were buried alive in Hoover Dam's concrete. It was too much trouble, the legends go, for anyone to fish them out. Almost certainly apocryphal, the tales nevertheless highlight the attitude that human life was expendable.

Before industry started amplifying human muscle with machines and hydroelectric power, Hoover Dam's workers might have labored in fields, on ships, or in stables. The women in the Triangle Shirtwaist Factory might have sewn at home with needle and thread, or worked in craftsmen's shops. Hard lives, but for many a cut above drudging in a sweatshop or toiling on a dreary, deadly construction project.

Industry brought higher standards of living and relief from backbreaking toil. Ironically, however, the muscle-power-amplifying transition made new demands on muscle; labor often grew unnatural and oppressive, sweat lost its healthy glow, and -- through accidents and overwork -- life was cut short. Although life got easier for many people, for many others, a tough life became tougher. Higher productivity often extracted higher human costs. As an old coal-mining song by Tennessee Ernie Ford goes, "Sixteen tons and what do you get? Another day older and deeper in debt.... I owe my soul to the company store."

Tough conditions, low pay, loss of personal identity and worth, divorce from the land. Bad news for many working people. But at least they had jobs. Others, like the desperate, hopeful migrants chronicled in John Steinbeck's Grapes of Wrath, wished they had work, any kind of work.

Job Extinction

The transition to industrialism engendered a new phenomenon: serial job destruction. This should not be surprising since the job as we know it was pretty much an industrial age invention.

In the agricultural age, people had roles on the farm; they went into professions like the clergy or doctoring; they apprenticed with blacksmiths or furniture makers. But their roles pretty much stayed put. Though choices were fewer, displacement was less frequent or nonexistent. Nobody got downsized off the farm. Few professional or crafts people were told, "Sorry, you're not needed any more; your function has been eliminated." Such things did start to happen as modern technology began in earnest to muscle in to muscle work:

- Tanners and cobblers were replaced by leather and shoe factories.
- Ditch diggers and excavators were replaced by backhoes and bulldozers.
- Pony Express riders, replaced by trains and delivery vans.
- Family farmers, replaced by agribusiness.

The list of jobs eliminated or made more efficient (translation, fewer workers needed for the same output) could go on and on. Of course, not everyone in a job category was replaced. For example, we still have a few ditch diggers. We're talking quantity.

As industrial machines and methods muscled in on our muscle work, some people like Andrew Carnegie and John Rockefeller got rich. Others enjoyed marginally better lives. And some got sucked into poorer times. Eventually, as the industrial age matured, times improved for those who learned new skills and made peace with machines and machine-like ways; but it took many decades.

More Than Occupational Disruption

People got hurt in their jobs and pocketbooks, but the displacement was more than vocational. Whole life-styles were chewed up and spat out. The nature of human interaction and freedom itself changed. There was plenty to adapt to. For example:

- People had to pick up their country stakes and move into factory towns and cities.
- Health was affected by poor working conditions, poor housing, and unnatural new forms of machine-related labor.
- Self-sufficiency waned as social forces imposed store-bought solutions.
- New media arising out of broadcasting and mass printing challenged minds unused to literate interaction or too poor to participate effectively.
- Although industrial development enriched many people, the changing role of money confused and indebted others. For example, in earlier time, when people built their own homes, they usually owned them; when industry started building houses for people, bankers held a mortgage. More than miners started owing their souls to somebody.

Today we forget how much was sacrificed to the God of industrial progress. As many occupations became automated, there was a general loss of broad know-how and comprehensive self-sufficiency.

In the new, machine-spawned cities and then in suburbia, people gradually lost the means or social permission to perform and enjoy basic activities that had been human hallmarks for centuries --

- how to cut, shape, and join wood.
- how to grow their own vegetables and grain.
- how to husband and butcher livestock.
- how to fish, hunt, and trap.
- how to make and repair their own tools.
- how to make their own music.
- how to make up and tell stories.

Mass advertising, the consumer, and new flavors of political action were born in this period. Making smooth, non-traumatic adjustments wasn't always easy. Many people suffered in subtle as well as substantial ways.

Did It Have to Be That Bad?

The transition to the industrial age displaced many people and created new kinds of hard times; but did the displacement have to be quite as disruptive as it was? Did life for so many have to get so bad?

There are ameliorating steps that society eventually took, and might have taken sooner.

35

For example:

- Government mandated new safety standards following the Triangle Shirtwaist Factory fire. If standards made sense then, why not earlier?
- Unemployment compensation was invented during Franklin Roosevelt's presidency. Why not during Wilson's?
- During World War II, women gained social permission to earn money in "male" jobs such as riveting and operating construction equipment. Why not during World War I or earlier?

There are also evasive actions that individuals might have made on their own (if they were prescient enough to see the trend), regardless of society's ameliorating steps. For example:

- If you were a seamstress who saw her job in jeopardy, you might have learned about the new sewing technology and gotten backing to set up a small sewing factory. You would have been a sweatshop owner, at least, rather than a sweatshop slave.
- If you were a worker in a carriage wheel shop, you might have seen the handwriting on the wall and learned something about the new-fangled horseless carriages -- opening a future as a mechanic.

The point: The pattern of transition that prevailed in the industrial age appears to be repeating itself now. As electronic systems muscle in on our mind work, displacement and the trauma of change loom. But there are ameliorating actions society can take; and there are adaptations each of us can make individually.

There's more to worry about, though, than the trauma of change. What about the end-game dangers?

Avoidable Ills of Industrial Society

No one quite set goals for the industrial age, though some painted glowing pictures. Edison, for example, looked out at a valley and said, " I am going to make it even more beautiful. I am going to dot it with factories." Technology was beautiful; and the whole idea was to augment human powers and thereby make life better. Industrial developments were supposed to --

- Make food more plentiful and varied.
- Increase the supply of necessities ranging from clothing to housing.
- Create new reservoirs of wealth.
- Raise levels of education and culture.
- Foster freedom and the pursuit of happiness.
- Secure the foundations for religious and personal aspirations.

The maturing industrial age did in fact produce solid results in all these areas. There were unintended negative consequences, though. In addition to the temporary negatives of the period of transition, these negatives are the rotten fruit that spoil the cornucopia once the transition is complete. These are the enduring end-game consequences, the hard-to-eradicate bad outcomes of the successful adoption.

They are the problems we face today. All of them might be less severe had we been prescient enough to predict and circumvent them. Obvious ones include --

- Environmental pollution.
- Suburban sprawl and urban decay.
- Dying family farms and junk-food diets.
- Inactivity, obesity, and stress-related health problems.
- Poverty and homelessness.
- Unemployment used as a tool for regulating the economy.
- Erosion of the company as stable employer.
- Alienation and rootlessness.
- Addiction to everything from tobacco to alcohol, sugar to drugs.
- Prevalence of crime, vandalism, and terrorism.

The augmentation of muscle power by itself did not produce these negatives. Rather, the negatives gradually accumulated as byproducts of an industrializing society, with causal tributaries of ecology, sociology, politics, greed, and myopia.

During previous decades, we might have done more to make such problems less extreme. For example:

- **The family farm didn't have to die.** Agribusiness didn't have to happen. Government policy created today's agricultural norm; public apathy let it happen. A vocal senator or an agrarian Ralph Nader could have sent us in another direction.

- **Lake Erie didn't have to almost die before we started cleaning it up.** With the right public attitude and policies, we could have kept it pure all along. Industrial pollution is a function of greed and haste. It was possible earlier, as now, to progress without mess.

- **Companies didn't have to evolve into revolving doors that churn expendable people.** There's no fix in sight, but one surely exists. After all, one sense of the word "company" is a group of interacting people (as, Shakespeare's company of players) in contrast to a legal fiction fronted by a logo and backed by money.

- **Terrorism didn't have to rear its ugly head so high.** With better foresight and foreign policy, we might have ameliorated the poverty

39

and oppression that feed resentment, desperation, and violence.

Of course it's easy to look back and say what might have been. The point is not to criticize the past but to steer toward a better future using our rear-view mirror. If we acknowledge that things might have developed even a little bit differently, we gain confidence for shaping the future. By spending even a little time thinking ahead, we can sidestep some of the negative consequences that might otherwise arise.

Industrial Possibilities Foregone

Society exploited the opportunities of muscle replacement well. Discoveries of scientists fed the imaginations of inventors, which triggered the schemes of entrepreneurs. The public, fast being reborn as consumers, did their part by purchasing the new machine-made clothes, living in the new mass-built homes, eating the new processed foods, and moving about in the new mechanical conveyances. Almost overnight, we ended up with today's mature industrial world: skyscrapers and airports, TV and shopping malls, global commerce and space flight.

No stone of industrial opportunity was left unturned, or so it would seem. But the world might have turned out far different than it has.

For example:

- **Lighter-than-air transport was big business until the Hindenburg exploded.** Then the industry suddenly deflated. Were it not for that accident, or if we had reacted differently to it by making the technology safer, zeppelins and blimps might dot our skies today. Our goods and many of our travelers might be wafted silently from here to there, resulting in fewer trucks and cars on our highways, fewer highways, and less air pollution.

- **Railroad technology might have developed to a much higher degree than it did.** The laws of physics or God did not dictate that once the auto became possible it had to be built in quantity. It did not have to be proliferated by the construction of roads and highways. Suburbia, spawned by the auto, did not have to sprawl over the landscape, squeezing farms and squashing villages. Suppose we had opted to forego the auto and push railroad transport. Instead of suburbia we might have close-knit communities at the end of railroad spurs. These would be like small cities without the sprawl that requires motorized transit to everything. People would live in closer proximity, as on a college campus. Cultural amenities would be within walking or biking distance. There would be smaller lawns and more shared green spaces.

41

R&D that went into autos would have gone into rail technology. We might have sleek, 200-mile-per-hour bullet trains; we might have ancillary pneumatic tubes swooshing goods from here and there.

- **While we seized the opportunity to increase the quantity of food, we missed the opportunity to improve its quality in equal degree.** Just because food could be processed didn't mean it had to be, at least not in the ways and to the extent it was. When our muscle power was multiplied by technology, it became possible to produce and deliver better, fresher, healthier foods of all types. It also became possible to refine the nutrition out of flour and extract sugar in its pure, health-degrading form. We seized the latter opportunity more than the former (both as consumers and producers). Our new industrial power gave us the ability to create a diverse, distributed agriculture; more food might be grown in and near the communities where it is consumed. Our industrial power also gave us the ability to banish food growing to Kansas, resulting in loss of freshness and requiring the use of preservatives. We went for the second option rather than the first. (Today faster transport and refrigeration allow us to enjoy fresh food from anywhere on the planet. We pay for it in expensive infrastructure and pollution from jet and truck exhaust.)

If we believe in free will, we must acknowledge that hosts of things might have turned out better based on the values, foresight, and courage of business leaders, politicians, scientists, engineers, and ordinary citizens. Missed opportunities abound, small as well as large. In 1858, Hamilton Smith patented the rotary washing machine. It took nearly 30 years for someone to invent a comparable machine to wash dishes. Delayed opportunity. The inventor, Josephine Cochran, is reputed to have exclaimed, "If nobody else is going to invent a dishwashing machine, I'll do it myself!"

Cochran's story leads us to the next point. In addition to missed opportunities of society-wide scope, millions of tiny, individual missed opportunities inhabit every era of change. If you see the big picture, you can take tiny steps in tune with the times.

Individual Paths Not Taken

Imagine yourself living at the early part of the transition to the industrial age. If you saw that the overarching trend was augmentation and replacement of human muscle power, you might have had an "aha!" The thing to do, you would have seen, was to stop trying to compete with your muscles; the thing to do was to develop skills involving thought and knowledge.

Narrow know-how would have been your direction. Develop expertise to stay ahead of the curve, specialized know-how to carve your place in the future and avoid excessive trauma of change.

It could have been specialized know-how of anything suiting your personality, skills, and situation. Specialized know-how of mechanical things such as mills, looms, engines, and conveyors. Specialized know-how of new industry-related procedures such as the perfection of repeatable steps, whether in factories, banks, or on fishing vessels. Specialized know-how of new ways to work a farm and increase crop yields.

If you made your living digging ditches, hated it, but couldn't imagine another occupation, you would have added specialized know-how to the task. Were there new and better shovels? Better ways to use a shovel to minimize strain and maximize productivity? New ways to organize others to dig ditches? New power-driven machines that could dig a lot faster?

Knowing that the big, general trend of the times was muscle augmentation and replacement, you would have stopped trying to compete with your muscle power alone. You would have "given up" gracefully and accentuated your higher human capabilities -- the use of your mind within a machine-related niche.

In the transition to the industrial age, specialized know-how was king. In the transition to the information age, it's the same but different. Something else reigns. While specialized know-how is still important, specialized know-how is the very thing that is now being augmented and replaced. That aspect of our minds is going into the electronic sphere. We need to make a mental adjustment of a new and different sort.

As the industrial era progressed, machines won out over labor in progressive waves of change that swamped some people while sweeping others to higher ground. Now, mental labor is the target of change. We need to keep our wits about us.

3

The Electronic
Brain Drain

Big Promise, Big Danger

We can move with speed, courage and exhilaration toward a world with enough for everyone. Or today's transition, pursued without course change, can be much worse than yesterday's; and the future we end up with could be just plain dreadful or non-existent.

A Personal Transition

Fresh out of high school, I wasn't emotionally or financially ready for college and needed a job, any job. One day I walked into the lobby of a modernistic, glass-and-concrete building that housed a defense contractor that produced guidance systems for aircraft. I asked the receptionist if they had any jobs. She asked what kind I wanted. I asked what kind they had. They did in fact need a reliable, bright kid who was a stickler for detail and didn't mind hard work. Ushered down a hall to a large room surrounded by private offices, I was introduced to the manager of engineering.

He pointed to a big, black calculating machine sitting on a high desk. "We need someone to punch in numbers," he said, explaining that the company's engineers developed many formulas with data sets that needed to be applied against them. My job would be to tap the numbers into the machine, hitting various function keys -- plus, minus, times and so on -- as directed by an instruction sheet. Then I would collect the narrow printout tapes and give them to the engineer requesting the calculations.

"You would have to do this all day long, every day," he said, pointing out that it could get tedious and that speed and accuracy were important. "Is this something you think you'd be good at, and would you like to do it?"

Nausea or maybe fear pressed at my diaphragm. I really needed a job, but should I take this one?

I hesitated. My whole future hung in the balance. If I took the job, maybe I would do well at it and be offered a better, less tedious job. Maybe they would really like me and give me financial help to get a college degree; maybe I would major in engineering and invent something awesome.... They'd pay me a regular salary; I'd have coins and bills in my pocket, more than I needed. Maybe, in a few months, I could buy a nice car.... Maybe, just maybe, there was a bright, beautiful girl working down the hall....

The nausea/fear did not abate. "No," I said, reluctantly but with relief, "I don't think so." I could do numbers, but didn't love them. I really needed the money, but not at the cost of my soul.

I tell this story for two reasons. First, that type of work is long gone. Human number crunching, along with slide rules, has disappeared into PC's and network-based engineering-support systems. Many other white-collar jobs have gone away, too, and continue to poof like soap bubbles.

Second, we should think twice, especially today, before subjecting ourselves to mindless mind work. For humanitarian reasons, it should be phased out like monotonous muscle work in sweatshops and on production lines. Implemented right, the e-brain drain can be a very good thing.

Serial Job Destruction

Our special concern today isn't just that jobs are going away. Our concern is that mind-work jobs are going away. Mind-work jobs of a boring, menial sort are disappearing first, followed by others higher on the I.Q. scale. Long term, this trend may reach a very satisfactory conclusion, but for those caught in the grinding, merciless gears of transition, it's a bit of an issue.

Because no one seems to know what new kinds of jobs could possibly replace those being downsized, off-shored, made more "productive" and streamlined out of existence.

The case of a woman I'll call Dahlia illustrates the point. The dilemma she exemplifies is all too common and becoming more so. Fresh out of high school in the 1960's, she worked as a switchboard operator for a New Jersey pharmaceutical company. Then she took a long sabbatical to raise three children. In 1991, when she sought to re-enter the workforce, she looked for a switchboard operator's job but could not find one. The function had been automated. Now callers were greeted by robotic Dahlia's that said, "Press one for sales, two for service... If you know your party's extension, enter it now...."

Dahlia landed a related job, though, as a directory assistance operator. Her employer was a contracting company that supplied services to the large, now deregulated telephone companies. All seemed well, but one day Dahlia became uneasy when she read an article about new technology that could understand speech and respond with information. Was her new occupation in jeopardy?

Dahlia's apprehension was justified. Between 1999 and 2001, several of her associates became victims of downsizing. The reason? Business was soft; her employer's customers didn't have as much need for operator services. And why was that?

Dahlia eventually learned that automatic voice recognition systems could now handle up to 50% of the requests people made for directory information. Only "problem" calls were shunted to real operators. To save money and keep competitive, the phone companies were eliminating human costs everywhere they could. Over 60 but without the means to retire, Dahlia began to worry and developed stress-related headaches.

The headaches of all directory-assistance operators will get worse, because new voice-response systems now being deployed can satisfy 70% of directory assistance requests, with the eventual goal of approaching 100%. An example is AT&T's new 800-number lookup service, powered by TellMe Networks, a startup that provides a range of voice-triggered services based on voiceXML technology. Dial 1-800-555-1212 and say the name of any company. If they have an 800 number, you'll get it sans human contact.

Dahlia's precarious job situation is of course no isolated case. A worldwide mental muscling-in is well underway and fast gaining momentum. Like machinery in the transition to the industrial age, electronic systems are simultaneously empowering us and displacing us. The promise is great but two drawbacks loom. They're the same drawbacks that prevailed as our muscles were augmented and replaced: the trauma of transition, and the prospect of unintended bad consequences at the mature end of the transition.

The trauma doesn't have to be excessive but could be for some people. Consider the uncertain prospects of people like Dahlia: Switchboard jobs -- gone. Directory assistance jobs -- going, gone. What's next, and next?

QUESTION:

If Dahlia were to lose her directory-assistance job, what action should she take?

- Look for a job as administrative assistant.
- Get a job as a supermarket checker.
- Acquire the skills to handle a more complex job, such as travel agent.

Dahlia might seek a job as administrative assistant, but more and more managers are tapping out emails instead of dictating letters, and many now do their own filing on PC hard drives or local area networks.

Supermarket checker? If willing to accept lower wages, Dahlia could start scanning groceries, but how many checkout aisles in your local market are now self-service, outfitted with scanners operated by the customer? None yet? One? Two? How many will there be in four or five years?

Dahlia would be well advised to move upward on the know-how scale, but many travelers now avail themselves of self-service Internet ticketing. Airlines have trimmed travel-agent commissions, too; they'd rather sell tickets directly via their own websites. As ordering services become more user-friendly on hand-held devices and voice-response systems, travel agents will be further challenged; so will people in many other occupations. The world is starting to run on automatic.

Where Are We Going to Fit?

What are people like Dahlia supposed to do? What's the right career path for her, for you? For many, the trauma of change is already acute and is likely to get a lot worse as the transition to the information age accelerates.

You don't want to be one of the grunts, like my father during the Depression, taking the brunt. With foreknowledge, you can sidestep much of the pain, and you have much to gain from supporting society-wide steps for easing the transition for everyone. If you occupy a position of influence in government, business, the media, technology, or education, you have a once-in-a-lifetime chance to make a difference.

We have more to concern ourselves with, though, than the trauma of change. The future we achieve after all that trauma might not be the promised utopia we hoped for. Depending on our foresight and actions right now, we could find ourselves blossoming in a golden age, or shriveling in a technosphere bent on making us irrelevant.

Let's consider two scenarios for how the information age might end up. The first, which seems probable if our myopia continues, is quite negative.

If we let the information age develop willy-nilly, or assume that industrial age thinking suffices to guide today's change, we could be in for big trouble. Putting on our negative-thinking hats, lets consider some of the possible traumas of change and a few of the longer-term rotten consequences.

UNPLANNED TRANSITION TO INFORMATION AGE
A NEGATIVE SCENARIO
Mind power is amplified but in destabilizing ways

Transition period	End result
Growth opportunity: People have the chance to develop mental skills that electronic systems aren't good at; and to invent new forms of business & social interaction. (This opportunity is not greatly seized in this scenario.)	**Positive outcome:** Solutions are found to many of the world's problems; higher standards of living are achieved; there is new leisure as electronic systems do the mental grunt work.... BUT ...
Trauma of change: Phone operators, secretaries, travel agents, engineers, middle managers, and others are displaced; the consumer mind is overwhelmed by advertising and media inflows. People in many walks of life suffer job loss or the need to change jobs often; incomes are interrupted; lifestyles are degraded while people "find themselves"; there is loss of self-esteem as work skills are devalued; millions get overstressed as they vainly chase new skill sets that race into obsolescence.	**Negative consequences:** At the mature end of the transition, there is severe unemployment with no good way for many people to earn a living; the knowledge-based wealthy contrast with the have-nots who lack intellectual property; freedom is compromised; inequality stimulates crime and terrorism; addiction and other social ills become epidemic; suicide rates soar; human and electronic mental functions blend and people as we know them are gradually replaced.

Today trauma is being experienced in all career categories. Low-level mental tasks, like looking up phone numbers, are being transferred into the technosphere first, with higher-level tasks close on their heels. If your income rests on college or grad school laurels, you might feel immune to impact, but you're not:

- Programs that now search legal databases can be augmented to offer advice. Once that happens, would you bother to consult a lawyer on routine issues? Already there are computer templates that let you write your own contracts or create your own will.

- Doctors explain the significance of symptoms and offer health advice. Now, so do many web sites. For example, several departments of health post extensive information on Lyme disease detection, prevention, and treatment -- including photos and descriptions of deer ticks and rashes. With such information, many a doctor's visit can be avoided. Even TV ads offer information for self-diagnosis, urging us to just ask our doctors for prescriptions. Robotic surgery is on the horizon.

- Ad agency personnel check rates in the various media, place ads, and track response rates. Already computers help perform many of these tasks. Now software exists that generates names for new products, supplementing and supporting

54

but also encroaching on the creativity of copy-writers and account executives.

- We'll always need programmers, anyway, to put stuff into electronic systems, right? Wrong! Programming is one of the hottest areas for automation. Software developers constantly look for ways to get more code out of fewer people. For example, researchers at the University of Texas at Dallas recently developed "AutoCoder: An Intelligent Assistant for Coding Protocol Data."

As higher-level know-how is incorporated into electronic systems, every profession will feel the impact, even thought-intensive ones such as spacecraft engineering or particle physics. Artificial intelligence (AI) development has been proceeding apace in oil exploration, aerospace, health and safety, medical diagnosis, stock market investing, defense, industrial production, and many other areas. One system uses AI to automate the layout of directories and catalogues. There are predictions that smart systems will soon be able to perform library research, digest the data, and present conclusions in written form. Even editors and authors are at risk!

Broadly defined, AI includes expert systems, game playing, natural language processing, neural networks, robotics, and other advanced applications. But upscale occupations are affected by ordinary electronics as well as sophisticated software. For example, $250,000-a-year radiologists have started to complain that some of their work is being offshored to foreign radiologists who will work for a tenth the pay. The global Internet allows U.S. hospitals to send electronic versions of X-rays for instant analysis anywhere on the planet. Other medical tasks ripe for offshoring or automation include pathology, patient monitoring, and remote robotic manipulation of microscopes or surgical instruments.

Trauma Beyond Our Occupations

We've focused so far on the impact of the electronic brain drain on our work and livelihoods. Here, we are challenged in the pocketbook as our mental skills are transplanted into technology. But being sidelined is not our only risk, for the smart technology will not leave us alone. Like a late-arriving Big Brother, it is starting to mess with our minds and lives. It is doing so in two key modes:

- **Media bombardment.** Increasingly, electronic intelligence is managing and dispensing everything from news and entertainment to public relations and advertising. The assault on our minds never stops. With new precision and a pervasiveness that rivals the physical environment, media bombardment can enlighten and liberate us, or dull our minds and confound our lives.

- **Interactivity.** Characterized by the Internet but not limited to it, interactivity is like the one-way flow of traditional media, except it's two-way. Information goes into the mind and then out, or into the system from the mind with some kind of response back to the mind. Back and forth, back and forth. This mental ping-pong is a byproduct of the over-arching trend -- the electronic brain drain. Networks and communication devices need to be "smart" to respond sensibly to the myriad inputs and responses of people. As with media bombardment, interactivity can augment our power and freedom, or wreck everything.

Let's look at media bombardment and interactivity in more detail.

Media Bombardment

Imagine a world that has been turned into a garbage dump. Look around you. In all four directions, horizon to horizon, there's nothing but trash, refuse, discarded items of all types, rubble, garbage. It's not so bad. If you poke around, you can find a few valuable things. A chicken bone with a bit of good meat on it. A piece of wire to pinch-hit for a missing button. Scraps of wood and plastic for repairing your makeshift hut.

Your material needs are satisfied, and things are looking up. New inflows of garbage seem to contain a greater variety of food scraps; there's more discarded clothing, more reusable fragments and junk of all types. Furthermore, you're totally free to go wherever you like, do whatever you want. Poke and pick and choose to your heart's content. Best of all, everything is free, totally free. But you complain, "I don't want to live in a garbage dump!" A fellow scavenger looks around and says, "What garbage dump?"

Another scavenger, an older one, remembers the early days when there were clear patches, before garbage engulfed everything. She shrugs. "What can you do?"

The Great Mind Dump

Thanks to the industrial age and the beginning phases of the information age, our minds have been partially converted into garbage dumps. It's not so bad; there are lots of good things among the trash. And there are plenty of clear patches -- parks of consciousness with clean fields and clear lakes, unspoiled forests of thought, pristine shores of uncluttered mental expanse. But they're shrinking.

Aliens looking down on us might marvel that we cover our buildings and clothing with writing telling us to buy things. TV commercials crowd out pro-gramming, logos never leave the screen, and content has been infected with product placements.

More than most people realize, the content of newspaper and magazine stories comes from press releases issued by organizations with a product or viewpoint to sell. If you want your children to get more than a sanitized view of history, you can't rely on today's textbooks; their content has been screened by the prevailing prejudices of state school boards.

Our minds are up for grabs. Everybody wants a piece of them: marketers, legislators and politicians, media giants seeking to extend their empires, factions of all types, and friends who want us to try their multilevel marketing products.

Advertising is almost everywhere and becoming ever-present as well as ever more global. The Schick or Budweiser ad ends, but when the movie resumes, the hero is drinking a Bud or shaving with a Schick. Public television and movie theatres didn't used to run ads. Now both do. There has been a proposal to raise Federal revenue by selling advertising space in national parks and historic sites (we might create new names such as "The Aetna Insurance Washington Monument"). Someone has even suggested devoting one side of our paper money to ads.

Advertising can, of course, be carried to absurd lengths. On the following page you'll find my list of the top ten far-out places for ads. Four of them have already been exploited by astute marketers.

Top ten far-out places for advertising:

(1) In Chinese fortune cookies. Why waste the space on second-rate advice and predictions when you could be pushing first-rate sneakers or breakfast cereal?

(2) In marriage ceremonies. Right before or after "I do" would be a good place to promote a major hotel chain or rental car service.

(3) On the backs of ski-lift chairs. Think of the long minutes of wasted attention. You could capture it to promote hot chocolate mix or accident insurance.

(4) In classic works of literature. They could be revised to include product placements. For example, instead of the clam and oyster chowder mentioned in the first chapter of Moby Dick, you could insert Campbell's® Chicken & Stars or Progresso® Beef Barley.

(5) Inside of moving elevators. Like trapped skiers, trapped skyscraper dwellers offer golden moments of virgin attention. Electronic displays could tout investments and fine dining on the way up, legal services and antacids on the way down.

(6) During police arrests. Lawbreakers need to be read their rights, so why not have the reading "brought to you by Budweiser®" or "… the law offices of Butler, Bates, and Bustout."

(7) On fruit. People eat millions of bananas, oranges, apples, and pears. Why waste the skin surface with measly stickers that just say Chiquita® or Sunkist®? Why not also push pizza, record labels, or long-distance service?

60

(8) In DNA. The coats of animals have colored patterns such as stripes or geometric shapes. What a waste! With a little genetic tinkering, you could have giraffes sporting the AT&T logo, or tigers displaying the letters "GE."

(9) In constellations of stars. Star patterns are arbitrary, in the eye of the beholder. Why should we teach our kids to see a horse (Pegasus) or a hunter (Orion), when we could teach them to see something with a monetary kick to it, like the Prudential® rock, or the Morton® Salt girl?

(10) In dreams. People spend about a third of their lives asleep. Think of the boost to the economy if we could tap all that wasted consumer attention! It wouldn't take much. Kids of all ages already walk around with gadgets plugged into their ears. We'd just have to convince them to keep the plugs in at night.

The already-exploited ad opportunities are 1 (not only are ads appearing in Chinese fortune cookies, but also on the formerly plain takeout boxes), 3 (ads have appeared on ski lift chair in Sweden for some time), 5 (a service called Captivate places ads for Johnnie Walker and other products in office locations including elevators), and 7 (California-based Fruit Label Company has sold fruit-skin space to movie promoters and online services).

There's no question that advertising is getting more pervasive, but it's also coming at us more deviously. On TV, advertising seems to be commandeering more and more airtime. Yet advertising is starting (apparently) to disappear in spots. In time the majority of programs might be "ad-free"; but don't be fooled. Product promotion will most likely be there stronger than ever, in disguise. Two popular programs -- *Queer Eye for the Straight Guy* and *Emeril Live* -- make extensive use of product placements. The *Queer Eye* team features grooming and other products in the process of shaping up their straight-guy subject. Emeril frequently adds Emeril Essence -- his spice mixture available in supermarkets -- to dishes during his cooking show. "Add a little more Essence ... Bam!"

Both Emeril and the Queer Eye team show rather than sell. It may be a more effective way to push product.

There's nothing inherently wrong with product placement, or with traditional advertising for that matter. They are simply alternative methods of moving the goods. The thing we need to consider is the *extent* to which our minds are being influenced. Some influence is essential for commerce; 24/7 influence is too much.

Furthermore, we need to be aware of when and how our minds are being massaged. And those of us who do the massaging need to focus on methods and messages that are benign as well as effective.

The current period of transition is the time to do this kind of thinking. Once we unleash the full power of the information age, traditional advertising and PR can become ten times more intrusive. But that doesn't have to happen. We can develop other business models and ways of influencing one another.

Product placement is a good start on exploring alternative methods. Two other possible approaches, among several, include --

- **Interactive product infomercials and lookup databases.** Unlike today's ads that "come at" people; these entities would wait for people to come to them. You're in the market for a car? You would "go to" a what-if car-buying database (with visual, auditory, and computational elements). There you would learn at your leisure everything you want to know about makes, models, operation, looks, color, safety, and price. Major automakers have already implemented rudimentary versions of this approach; so has Consumer Reports. (These recessive ads may never replace traditional "at-you" ads, but may help reduce their number.)

- **Enhanced word of mouth.** Books become best sellers mostly through word of mouth. Publishers lack the big ad bucks available to sellers of soap or soft drinks. Suppose adverting were suddenly abandoned. Marketers could seek buyers through increased sampling or person-to-person methods such as network marketing. (Advertising won't go away, but imagining its absence can stimulate us to imagine other possibilities and make advertising less invasive and pervasive.)

Tomorrow's mental environment is not automatically destined to become ever more cluttered and trashy. Media began, we should remember, as speech, theatre, literature, knowledge, and information. Influence gradually crept in, but we can shove it back and make it more subservient.

Interactivity

Interactivity is like traditional media except it's two-way; back and forth rather than unidirectional.

Our whole culture is going interactive, but this trend will not eliminate hyper-commercialism. Far from it. Interactivity can be even more commercial and controlling than traditional one-way media, in spite of the new ability to click and choose.

At present interactivity is a small, almost trivial phenomenon compared to what it will become. Click on a web hyperlink and get a page of information back; enter a search term and find out something new; send an email and get an email back. Great, but it's only the infancy of tomorrow's hyper-interactivity. Everything's going interactive -- not just on the Net but in homes, on highways, in stores, in offices and factories, in schools and entertainment venues, in politics and culture and international affairs.

Tomorrow's interactivity will involve interacting with just about everything, not just web pages or email.

We'll be interacting with robotic systems, but the robots are joining us stealthily, in disguise.

QUESTION:

What will the typical robot of the future look like?

- 3CPO, the humanlike robot in Star Wars.
- A realistic humanoid modeled after someone like Julia Roberts or Tom Cruise.
- A refrigerator.
- A phantom.

There will of course be robots that approximate people and look like specific individuals, but they're not going to be the prime robots we'll be interacting with.

Our environment is being changed not by the sudden appearance of big, visible things, but by the steady, persistent encroachment of little things. A new chip here, a new chip there. A new bit of code here, another new bit there. The typical robot of the future will look like your refrigerator because it will be your refrigerator ... and your microwave oven ... and your front door ... and your furnace and kitchen sink ... and even your driveway and vegetable garden.

Many consumer devices -- washers and dryers, stereo systems and some lawn mowers -- already have chips in them that perform the functions previously performed by knobs, dials, and timers, not to mention homeowners. Do you still have to add bleach to your washer at just the right time during the cycle? Then you've got a very old model.

Most of our common mechanical devices are rapidly taking on new "mental" functions -- those requiring calculation, sensing, adjustment, low-level decision making, and response to emergency conditions. Today's cars already contain microchips controlling everything from ignition to braking to problem detection. Experimental cars that drive themselves have already been built; some steer themselves on stretches of California highway, and today you can buy a model that will parallel park itself.

If you chose "phantom," above, you may have been envisioning your future chauffeur, a phantom presence like the absent pilots in today's military reconnaissance planes. Jeeves, your coming chauffeur, will not be a robot sitting in the driver's seat, but your car itself.

Soon most of the everyday things that surround us will be electronically augmented or identified, including cans of tomatoes and cartons of eggs (with affixed radio frequency identification or RFID chips). We'll be interacting with all these things, but just how?

Since, unlike media bombardment, interactivity involves a two-way interplay of initiatives, freedom and human empowerment should be the consequences. That's true, but "should" doesn't always happen. For example, some DVD's are programmed to disable user controls during the commercials that precede the movie. You can't fast forward or choose a movie scene; you're trapped until the commercial ends. Now imagine the commercial messages and controls that could be programmed into your smart refrigerator, jogging shoes or electric service.

The positive end-state of interactivity can be an unprecedented, supportive form of human synergy and control. Unless we take care, though, the rise of media-controlled interactivity could leave us in a distressing condition: manipulated, isolated, or both.

Rotten Fruit in Tomorrow's Cornucopia

The negatives we've discussed could be temporary -- here just for a while, like sweatshop labor during the transition to the mature industrial age -- then gone. At the end of the transition to the information age, after a bit of painful adjustment, we could all be doing what we love, thinking perfectly clearly, and enjoying fulfilling, free lifestyles. On the other hand, some of the end-game fruit could be quite rotten, just as we're now living with rotten as well as wholesome fruit of industrialization. For example:

- **Unemployment could be chronic.** With intelligent systems doing most of the work, most people might have little means of proving their worth. This large population will raise tough questions for those who still have jobs. Should government support the non-productive? Do they deserve more than subsistence income?

- **A counterproductive caste system could develop** -- a wealthy minority who control the infrastructure and intellectual property, versus everybody else.

- **The minds of millions could resolve into a mush** as flows of commercial media gush out of control, with few people able to distinguish between advertising and entertainment, news or public relations. We already see signs of this in the public apathy to today's hyper-commercial TV and Washington's accelerated spin cycle.

- **Freedom could be degraded** as more and more information about us is stored in the network -- controlled by others, not us, and used to influence us, not help us.

- **Electronic crime, conventional crime, and terrorism could rage out of control,** inflamed by inequality, feelings of being left out, and gross disparities in wealth.

Such unintended outcomes would be quite distressing and bleak. The core trend, remember, is transference of mental functions into electronic systems. What happens at the far end of the trend? What happens if and when electronic entities become smarter than we are, more adept and responsive, more skilled in making decisions? What good are we to them at that point? What happens if and when some of us incorporate chips, cyber prosthetics, and artificial intelligence code into our bodies, and others don't? Internecine war? Genocide?

The extinction of the human race might be considered OK by some if what's left is a new, better species. If our electronic creations develop higher consciousness or if they come alive in better, brighter ways (like the bright robots in Steven Spielberg's movie, *AI*), our death might be acceptable -- a sacrifice for better "children." But what if the smart entities end up as nothing more than intricate zombies? What if the technosphere remains dark and dead, with nary a conscious being in sight?

There are many other possible scenarios, some of them not so bad, some of them pretty good. *Here's a great one:*

CONSCIOUS TRANSITION TO INFORMATION AGE
A POSITIVE SCENARIO
Mind power is amplified along fruitful avenues for all

Transition period	End result
Growth opportunity: People have the chance to develop mental skills that electronic systems aren't good at; and to invent new forms of business and social interaction. (This opportunity is greatly seized in this scenario.)	**Positive outcome:** Expanding consciousness and aliveness become the goals of life on earth. People and society evolve in desirable ways; a golden age blossoms. Human intelligence and aliveness are never exterminated but expanded through and with electronic intelligence.
Trauma of change: Administrative assistants, travel agents, engineers, managers, doctors, professors, and others are displaced; the consumer mind is threatened. BUT ... the trauma is minimized through public policy and private initiatives. New more stable company forms are invented; and new ways are found to compensate people. The media evolves in supportive ways.	**Negative consequences controlled:** Undesirable developments are minimized through foresight, astute monitoring, and application of caring intelligence to fix problems before they spiral out of control.

If we engage our higher mental capabilities -- our metamind -- and if we set good goals for the information age, foresee and prevent the major negative consequences, minimize the trauma of change, and seize growth opportunities aggressively and wisely, we can emerge from the transition OK. In fact, we can come out of it spectacularly.

The Importance of a Positive Vision

What kind of goals should we target? If you want to make it to the other side of a chasm, conservative, small steps won't do. In fact, they're lethal. To clear such a divide, one must make a grand leap. Our goals should be as big as the chasm is wide.

Our grand leap starts with changing an age-old assumption that resides deep in all of us: that there isn't enough to go around. We believe, because it has always been true, that only some of us can survive and live well, but all can't.

The conviction that scarcity will always be with us causes us to perpetuate a society with haves and have-nots. And of course we'd all rather be haves -- if not for our own sakes, then for the sake of our families. Also, we figure, how can we help others if we don't have the means to do so, which requires the will and aggressiveness to become haves.

This assumption of scarcity, arising from the fact of scarcity, gives rise to heated competition, which results in war and destruction.

We can now start to change the assumption of scarcity, because, thanks to technology, we now have the means to end scarcity, and with it, the contention that results in today's social conflict, militarism, terrorism, and crime.

Scarcity can be all but eliminated within the first half of this century. If we're not visibly on track for ending it soon, the world is likely to self-destruct through technology's increasing disempowerment of the middle and lower classes.

So our grand leap must land us beyond the dark crevice of yesterday's assumptions and behaviors. We must start assuming that there can soon be enough for everyone, and set about to make it so.

If there was ever a time to end world hunger, this is it. If there was ever a time to help third-world nations free themselves of oppression and poverty, this is it. If there was ever a time to release the genius of all children, this is it. If there was ever a time to root out the real causes of substance abuse, this is it. If there was ever a time to make Earth into a garden and reach new heights in science, culture, and human relationships, this is it. Such goals may seem unrealistic, but without them we'll fall short, right into the chasm.

Such goals are in fact technically feasible. Think of the resources we have at our disposal: billions of interacting people supported by mind-extending infrastructure that is growing exponentially. What might we not do -- we, the mighty, ever-smarter global mind?

Today a computer that you can hold in one hand is more powerful than a roomful of early computers; and if current trends continue, in 20 years the power of a supercomputer could fit in your pinky ring. Now think of ever more powerful computers linked together over the surface of the whole Earth, forming trillions of connections like neurons in a gigantic brain. More and more human know-how pumped into the system. More and more tasks done automatically, more and more problems solved with less and less effort, more and more innovations, more and more wealth and harmony.

Minimizing the Trauma & Staying on Top

If a positive scenario such as this is to have a chance, it will be necessary for humans to stay in control by moving up to a higher mental level, metamind. No matter how extensively electronic systems muscle in to our mental work or invade our personal lives, we will need to maintain and magnify our supremacy. Not just a self-selected few but the broad population. Harmonious, synergistic cultures require full participation; beehives thrive because all the bees belong.

Society could self-destruct if too many find they have no place. Severe trauma of change won't be tolerated. People won't play occupational musical chairs for long without striking back at the system. Today's employment practices, like today's fast-morphing companies, are showing signs of obsolescence.

Structures designed for the industrial age may be unworkable for the fast-paced, accelerating information age.

73

New thinking is needed here. It won't do to treat people like replaceable parts, passive sponges, or puppets on interactive strings.

Already traumatic for the employed as well as the displaced, the transition to the information age doesn't have to keep on hurting so much. The hurt doesn't have to get worse. Steps can be taken to move ahead positively and with ease in spite of moving faster. Fresh approaches are needed and we can develop them.

Opportunities Not to Be Missed

When the fabric of society changes, it's futile to hold on to old patterns. When modern plumbing became available, it would have been silly to put your new bathroom in an outhouse. We don't want to miss chances to restructure society in ways appropriate for the information age.

For example, today's suburban communities and cities may no longer be the ideal form for living and interacting in a mind-powered society. New living-working complexes, such as the "intercommunity" (discussed later in this book), might profitably be explored. Business parks and office buildings may no longer be the ideal environments to support work at a time when wide-ranging interaction is the thing that brings results. Telecommuting may be part of a better way, but only a part. There are additional possibilities discussed later in this book.

Money and compensation cry out for re-examination, too; let's not miss the opportunity to reinvent them. In the industrial age, value as defined by the dollar or pound was relatively stable, and compensation rewarded production-style contributions. In the information age, value flits and flies all over the place; and the network supersedes the production line.

In the network of a human brain, which neuron deserves compensation for transmitting which impulse that triggers which thought? It's impossible to tell. All the neurons work together to spark all the thoughts, and all require and deserve nourishment. Maybe we don't need traditional money at all anymore; maybe there are better vehicles for stimulating and regulating information-age interactions. Plastic and electronic transfers have already altered money's form and fluidity.

Transportation, food production, health care, education, law, the media -- these and other areas are ripe for structural change or reaffirmation. We have an unprecedented chance to look at every aspect of our physical, economic, social, and political systems and make sure they're best for the world that's emerging.

The Biggest Opportunity of All

A positive, successful transition to the information age calls for yet another reexamination. This one may be the most important of all. Since electronic systems are taking over many of our mental tasks, we need to shift to others, but which ones?

QUESTION:

Which of the following jobs is least likely to be replaced or impacted by electronic technology?

- Accountant
- Lawyer
- Auto mechanic
- Standup comic
- Physics professor
- Dietician
- Salesperson

Electronic systems are great at numerical functions including tax computations and developing profit & loss statements. They're good at looking up facts and dispensing data, including legal, dietary and scientific information. Computer-assisted instruction is coming on strong, especially in structured subjects such as physics. Electronic devices already diagnose problems with cars; and robotic systems that assemble cars may soon have counterparts in repair shops.

The standup comic probably has the greatest job security. So where does that leave us? The answer lies in an examination of our mental strengths and weaknesses compared to the strengths and weaknesses of electronic intelligence. We need to shift to areas of mentality where we outshine our creations. What are we really good at? And where do computers, networks, and electronic devices leave us in the dust?

WHAT MENTAL TASKS ARE WE BETTER AT?

Humans excel at ...	E-systems excel at ...
METAMIND **MICRO SKILLS** 1. Basic thinking skills and symbolism. **MACRO SKILLS** 2. Conscious monitoring and control (perceptual and motor). 3. Hypothesizing. 4. Creativity and imagination. 5. Subjective decision making. 6. Social skills. 7. Responsibility (valuing, love, and pursuit of ethical objectives).	**DEFINED OPERATIONS** ● Number crunching and routine logic. ● Mass storage and retrieval. ● Remote sensing and control. ● Structured or routine decision making. ● Control of repetitive processes. ● Simple or labor-intensive instruction.

Our big differentiator is our aliveness. We see objects, feel breezes, have feelings, develop intentions, and picture possibilities -- all in living color. We're conscious. Furthermore, unique among all creations, we're meta-conscious or self-aware. We know we're alive and can control our thoughts and actions. We possess the magic of reflection; we're aware of our awareness and therefore in charge.

We may one day succeed in producing electronic consciousness and even meta-consciousness, but don't count on it happening any time soon. We don't even know yet what our own consciousness is, what its limits and interconnections are, or where it comes from.

Even if we could create machine consciousness, there is no compelling need to do so. Our machines don't have to be alive to extend our minds spectacularly and do great things for us. The transfer of specialized know-how is transition enough for the information age (unless we're bent on replacing ourselves).

Our reflective form of awareness permits a number of other mental functions that machines can't attack well if at all. We're great at sensory perception while computers linked to sensors struggle to form composite impressions. We laugh, feel pleasure and sorrow, love. No competition at all from our machines.

We just naturally imagine and dream up new possibilities; electronic systems merely correlate and combine. Only we make choices based on subjective as well as logical considerations. Computers are limited by logic and fact. Within complex environmental and social contexts, we can easily dream up speculations about why things happened. Electronic intelligence can't even start to guess, though it can induce and deduce within data structures accessible to it. Finally, we have social skills. Electronics, no contest.

Electronic systems beat us hands down in defined, structured areas where we're weak or get bored. Even those of us who are good at math and logic do it much slower than electronic systems and lack patience for much of it at a time. Human memory, too, has limits. You probably can't call to mind all the phone, fax, and email addresses of all your friends and associates, whereas the Internet can "remember" all that plus Library of Congress with ease. Human sensory perception can't be beat, but is limited in range. Internet-connected cameras, microphones, and monitoring devices can supply input from thousands of miles away. Electronic intelligence is great at repetitive tasks such as monitoring chemical processes or managing lab tests. Nothing can beat a good human teacher, but simple instructions, drill, and reminders require only dull persistence; electronic systems are great at that.

Success Strategy for the Information Age

We can overcome the negative possibilities by emphasizing our meta-conscious or hyper-human qualities. Let electronic systems take the structured, repetitive stuff. Specialize in and perfect the human qualities that set us apart: consciousness including very conscious modes of perception, emotion, creativity, and the ability to interact with other people.

Our opportunity is to get better and better at being alive and to stop sacrificing others in the old notion (generally true until now) that our survival depends on it. Perfecting our human qualities requires moving from the prevailing win-lose paradigm (based on assumed scarcity) to a new win-win paradigm (based on emerging sufficiency). This will involve honing a special, rather rare form of conscious control: broad responsibility (to be discussed later).

Magnifying our humanness is the winning strategy for the long-haul transition to the information age. It won't always produce tangible results in the near term, however. Industrial-age win-lose approaches linger. Lower-level "production-line" abilities, dog-eat-dog competitiveness, and specialized know-how continue to be prized. They're systematically being replaced, though, and attitudes are changing.

Longer term, the good news is that the route to success is to become even more human than we already are. We can leave the boring things to the computers, the networks, and the gadgets. We can let them handle the routine choices, the record keeping. We can let them store the data and remember the details.

As advanced hyper-human beings, we can use the technosphere as a facile but servile extension of our own mentality -- auxiliary memory, math whiz on call, network gofer, receptionist, accountant, remote eyes and ears, and sentry on the lookout for new developments as we alert it to our needs.

Employment ads still seek people to just answer phones, type letters and file papers, or repeat the same sales pitch over and over. There's still a heavy demand for people with "5+ yrs prgr'g dBase III db's." Routine and narrow know-how prevail. However, ads also seek people who are "creative problem solvers who can roll with punches." Times are changing.

While continuing to peddle our more replaceable mental skills, it is essential to hone our human qualities -- to become more creative, social, and emotionally connected. It pays to make ourselves more visionary and develop more big ideas. It pays to become more decisive and make more things happen. Above all, it pays to brighten our aliveness. Polishing up our human qualities will help us later and help us now, however machine-replaceable our current tasks may be.

This mental-development direction won't point with precision to where the jobs are. It won't tell you exactly what new jobs are going to materialize tomorrow. Clues are available, though. Stay tuned.

The honing of consciousness is also the winning strategy for improving the general, non-work areas of our lives. It helps free us from influences that limit our possibilities and dim our aliveness.

The Possible End State

If we make the great leap successfully, the other side of the chasm could be a near paradise. Through multiplied intelligence, we might live in a world where --

- Everyone has enough to eat.
- Discussion and problem solving have replaced global violence.

- Nurturing of the environment and wise use of resources have won out over wasteful consumption and production that pollutes.
- The necessities of life are no longer tied to traditional unfulfilling jobs.
- Companies have bifurcated into mostly non-human operational infrastructure, and into mostly-human task forces for creating the next new things.
- Everyone who wants to, from toddler to senior, learns like lightning -- via electronic systems, other people, and direct observation.
- Science probes deeper and deeper into the universe, the atom, and reality.
- Culture thrives as never before; music, art, dance, and theater enjoy a renaissance; wholly new art forms engage the senses, emotions, and thought.

In addition, increased consciousness -- our main springboard for leaping the present chasm -- is also our main goal. Nobody knows exactly what mature ultra-reflective consciousness might be like when shared by many people together. Some kind of wonderful. It's an end state our ever-smarter electronic systems can help us achieve; it's a state we're made to experience.

4

The Technogreed Tsunami

Undercurrent that's Overwhelming Us

A special form of greed, technogreed, propels the brain-drain trend in its destructive direction. Carrying the old assumption of not enough for everyone, today's leading brand of selfishness employs technology for self-preservation and advancement.

Few pursue technogreed with gross calculation. They (we) do it to secure the future and gain protection from threats of all sorts, real and imagined.

The worst offenders, the grand masters of techno-greed, are certain captains of industry who leverage technical and economic trends to amass billions while impoverishing millions and jeopardizing the planet.

Most of us in industrialized countries are guilty of technogreed to some degree. It's an understandable but dangerous trait; we need to replace it with an equally strong but positive impetus. Metamind, bolstered by the assumption of enough for everyone, can bring about the *fact* of enough for everyone, and that can counter the overheated impulse to stock one's pantry.

Technogreed, while lining the pockets of many, is raising dark clouds for all. We should be experiencing historical déjà vu, because we're starting to feel the same empowerment but suffer the same trauma felt by laborers, farmers, and craftsmen when machine power extended muscle power but extracted the livelihood from labor. Except now it's mind power that's flowing out of us and into our tools. And the consequences could be much more traumatic, even terminal.

Back then, people adjusted by moving from labor-intensive jobs to know-how jobs. That won't work this time, because know-how tasks are the very kind being usurped.

We need a new strategy for the new transition, and we should not expect an improving economy to restore the quantity and mix of yesterday's employment.

As recently as 1900, it took almost 40% of the workforce to grow America's food. Today, thanks to progressive mechanization, it takes less than 2%.

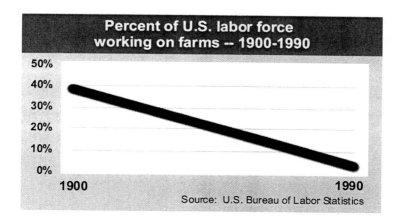

Percent of U.S. labor force working on farms -- 1900-1990

Source: U.S. Bureau of Labor Statistics

Farming Foretells the Future

As farms became well-oiled machines, farm hands went to factories and offices requiring new skills. (Those who stayed in agriculture had to master new skills in mechanics, bioscience and economics.)

Blue-collar work has retraced much of farming's downward trajectory. According to the U. S. Bureau of Labor Statistics, goods-producing workers decreased from 38% of the non-farm workforce in 1940 to 17% in 2003. Service-producing workers now account for more than 83% of the non-farm workforce. It's not hard to imagine goods production soon joining farming in the less-than-2% club. At that time, the service sector would, by today's definition, boast more than 98% of the non-farm workforce. But there's a problem.

As information technology automates white- and blue-collar functions alike, elements of most jobs *as we*

85

know them are being transferred into electronic systems. By 2100 it is possible that fewer than 2% of the U.S. non-farm workforce will be needed to handle today's quantifiable, structured know-how functions in factories, offices, stores, professional suites, hospitals, research labs, and universities.

Percent of U.S. labor force producing goods vs. services -- 1940-2003

Source: U.S. Bureau of Labor Statistics

To earn their keep, Americans -- like yesterday's farm hands -- will need to move on by moving up. But to what? And if a labor shortage materializes, how can we best accelerate the flow of tasks into automated systems -- while empowering people to accentuate the skills only humans have, without employment churn?

If know-how work is being taken over by ever-more-sophisticated tools, what's left for people to do?

Outflow of Know-how Work

White-collar know-how work is fast going the way of manufacturing and farming. Transferred bit by bit into electronic systems, these jobs are getting smaller and many if not most will eventually go away entirely. Ideally, they will be replaced by a new class of jobs that has yet to be named: work involving hard-to-automate hyper-human skills that go beyond know-how. But that remains to be seen, as does the path to achieving it.

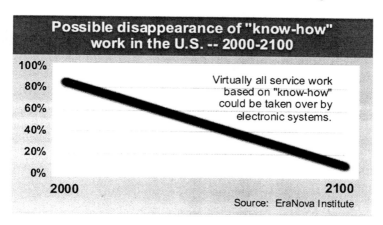

Possible disappearance of "know-how" work in the U.S. -- 2000-2100

Virtually all service work based on "know-how" could be taken over by electronic systems.

Source: EraNova Institute

Due to the transfer of human functions into logic-savvy systems, many jobs are on the way out or have already bitten the dust. Obvious examples include:

- **Typesetter** (extinct thanks to word processing and page layout software).
- **Receptionist** (replaced by electronic switches, "press 1 for sales").

- **Directory-assistance operator** (fast being replaced by automated alternatives such as AT&T's new voice-response directory service, available at 1-800-555-1212).
- **Personal secretary / administrative assistant** (a dying breed, except for those serving the "big boss," thanks to word processing, email, electronic filing, and online calendars).
- **Various clerks, number crunchers, proofreaders, etc.** (widely replaced by spreadsheets, decision support systems, and spellchecking).

Such occupations could soon be as rare as scrivener or lamp lighter. According to the Labor Department's Bureau of Labor Statistics, many service-sector jobs have lost people during the 1993 -- 2003 decade, when they should have gained 19% just to stay even with the overall increase in the workforce. Examples include:

- **9,700 fewer travel agents** -- down 7% (made more efficient but fewer needed thanks to online booking).
- **5,200 fewer people working in gas stations** -- down 4% (fewer attendants needed thanks to self-service pumps with credit-card readers).
- **7,600 fewer personnel in commercial banking** -- down 1% (made more productive but less in demand by electronic systems, Internet banking options, ATM's, and bank consolidation).

- **300 fewer people in book publishing** -- down a fraction of a percent when the category should have added thousands to stay "even" (focusing more narrowly on selection and distribution as editing and publishing functions are relinquished to PC-wielding authors and agents, and to on-demand publishing services).

- **7,600 fewer musical groups and artists** -- down 22% (out of demand thanks to recordings and computerized backup music for a single live performer).

Media and publishing sectors seem to be playing musical chairs. On the losing-chair side, the Bureau of Labor Statistics reports that 47,600 fewer people work in newspaper publishing -- down 11% (thanks to automation, consolidation, and a public that prefers to listen and watch).

On the gaining-chair side, the decade netted 45,200 new jobs in radio and TV broadcasting. The increase, however, lags behind the nation's population growth -- only 16% versus the 19% labor-force growth. (Don't count on much TV and radio job creation in the decade ahead. "Broadcasting automation" is hot; and equipment is being installed to simplify content creation, integration, ad insertion, and studio management. Then there's job-squeezing media consolidation.)

The decade brought 133,000 more lawyers and employees in legal offices. But the increase was only 15%, a relative loss compared to the 19% labor-force increase. (In spite of lawyers, lawyers everywhere, a real live one is not always necessary now that it's so easy to download fill-in forms for a will or contract).

Some key job categories not individually tracked by the government are also under assault by the electronic brain drain:

- **Sales representative** (needed for complex sales but optional for orders that can be placed via automated systems on the phone or Internet).
- **Middle manager** (still needed but in fewer layers, thanks to information systems that link end-point production or customer data directly into reports available to higher management).
- **Information technology professional** (still needed in the U.S. but often replaceable by cheaper overseas pros thanks to Internet-based systems that make offshoring easy).

Some job categories have outpaced overall labor-force growth during the decade. However, professionals in these fields should not feel immune from brain-drain forces. Example include:

- **255,700 more workers in accounting and bookkeeping services** -- up 39%. (The increase would be even greater were it not for fast-improving do-it-yourself accounting and tax-preparation software. The complexity of accounting, requiring human intervention, stems in large part from the changing constraints of nitpicking laws. Once smart systems negotiate the intersection of law with accounting and bookkeeping procedures, the need for human number-crunchers will wane).

- **589,600 more physicians and medical office personnel** -- up 42%. However, the number began to decline after 2001, down 19,200 or 6% between then and 2003. (Optimum health may always require human caring and consciousness. However, doctors are becoming optional for prevention and minor maladies thanks to information and self-diagnosis tools readily available on the Net and in drugstores. Doctor downsizing could accelerate with advances such as medical artificial intelligence and increasingly robotic diagnostic and surgical procedures.)

- **409,700 more people working in colleges and universities** -- up 46%. (Hopefully real, live people will always be needed for motivation and creative interaction. But look for human educators and their staffs to give way to information-delivery systems for repetitive course material or learning that requires access to large databases of hard-to-remember facts).

Today cost pressures dominate executive decision making, and the most cutable costs are people costs.

White Collars in the Crosshairs

In today's major corporations, white-collar jobs are being targeted with a vengeance. The reason, of course, is to increase productivity and the bottom line in order to remain competitive and to provide ever-increasing value to customers and stockholders, not to mention senior management. The targeting, made possible by electronic technology, is materializing in three key forms: corporate restructuring, offshoring, and inter-company systemization.

▶ **Corporate restructuring.** Justified by economic pressures, competition, or the need to play the merger game, restructuring is made possible by office automation, global networks, computers and electronic gadgets of all types. Fewer and fewer people can do the work of many. The current global torrent of acquisitions, spin-offs, realignments and downsizings is likely to continue for as long as information technology keeps on advancing.

▶ **Offshoring.** Thanks to modern communications, additional white-collar tasks are being outsourced to bargain-rate foreign suppliers. According to Forrester Research, an estimated 3.3 million U.S. high-tech and service jobs will go overseas between 2000 and 2015, most to India but many also to China, the Philippines, Malaysia, Vietnam, and elsewhere. Corporate savings are sizeable. According to Paaras Group, in 2002 --

92

- **A software programmer** in India cost $10,000 per year; in the U.S., $66,100.
- **A mechanical engineer** in India, $5,900; in the U.S., $55,600.
- **An accountant** in India, $5,000; in the U.S., $41,000.

Anything that can be done by telephone or PC is a candidate for offshoring, including sales, customer-care, web design, legal research, and editing. Those who supervise others are not exempt. According to the Forrester study, 288,281 U.S. management jobs will go to foreign pros by 2015.

An increasing number of America's largest corporations have moved white-collar jobs offshore: American Express, AT&T, Microsoft, Delta Air Lines, Oracle, Novartis, Hewlett-Packard, Dell, AOL Time Warner, HSBC, Texas Instruments, JP Morgan Chase, and many others.

According to Frontline World, over half of the Fortune 500 have already participated in offshoring. Others are expected to follow suit, and current participants are going for a second dip. For example, Oracle has announced plans to double its workforce in India, to 6,000.

Corporations often offshore indirectly by subcontracting to service firms such as eFunds of Scottsdale, Arizona, which in turn hire low-wage foreign pros. For example, Charles Schwab recently moved part of its information technology operation to a contractor in Bangladore, India.

In time the jobs lost to foreign workers will be lost by those workers as well, to all-electronic solutions. The job-sucking brain drain is a two-stage process that mirrors what has been happening with manufacturing. First, millions of jobs are given to low-paid foreign workers, then the functions are transferred to even cheaper people-free systems such as automated factories. Offshore, then offpeople.

In October, 2003, I kidded our big-company CEOs by developing a list of the top ten reasons to offshore their positions along with those of their high-tech and service employees. It was featured in **Training Magazine, COMPUTERWORLD** and other publications.

Top ten reasons to offshore the CEO position:

(1) Plenty of biz school grads in Pakistan, India, and China will gladly do the CEO thing for about $13,500 a year. That's a $13,486,500 saving per company now paying their big guy $13.5 million.

(2) Instead of laying off 346 underpaid people, you can save as much by laying off a single overpaid one.

(3) Until now only CEOs could play the layoff game. Now corporate boards can join the fun, since the only employee they can ax is the CEO.

(4) Since white-collar as well as blue-collar jobs are going overseas, the boss might as well be where all the workers are.

(5) American CEOs deserve the same life-changing help as everyone else: outplacement; career counseling; and skill training in growth areas like hospital work, fast-food service, and auto sales.

(6) If the nation's top 500 CEOs were all laid off, unemployment would go up only about 0.0056%, to 9,000,500.

(7) The new foreign CEOs will have tax equity with their workers, since neither will have to pay income taxes to Uncle Sam.

(8) Instead of supporting expensive vacation homes and yachts, you'd only have to support vacation yurts and sampans.

(9) Output per dollar cost will zoom as big CEO salaries are eliminated. The boost in productivity will eventually create new, better jobs (they say).

(10) CEOs will start bonding with regular people by sharing their experiences and lifestyles. Out on the street and minus their millions, they will make lots of new friends.

NOTE: While *offshoring* is a recent term applied to white-collar outsourcing, the practice does not differ from exporting manual work. In two years following July 2000, 2.6 million manufacturing jobs were lost.

▶ **Inter-company systemization.** Within the next decade, many corporate jobs will be impacted by the deployment of "Web Services." This new software technology automates interactions between companies, on the heels of software that has already automated functions within individual companies. Workers in jeopardy include --

- Purchasing agents
- Internal sales people
- Customer service representatives
- Stock clerks
- Accounting personnel
- Paper pushers of all types

The key benefit touted for Web Services is automated interactions that yield savings in time and cost. Translation: bigger bottom lines through smaller payrolls.

The rollout of Web Services appears to be substantial. A survey of 796 medium to large companies, conducted April, 2002, by The FactPoint Group and Outsource Research Consulting, indicated that nearly half are piloting or deploying Web Services. First to go will be the lowest-level, most routine white-collar jobs; then office-support and middle-management positions will be on the block. Upper management, already stressed by recent reorganizations, will be further pressed as well.

The job dislocation examples cited here are relatively minor compared to the employment impact that may be on the horizon two, three and four decades hence. It is possible that we are less than 5% "in" to the information age in terms of the mental functions that may be usurped by electronic intelligence.

Look for know-how service jobs to join the less-than-2% club as soon as mid-century.

IT Job Losses Lead the Way

While information technology (IT) is a key cause of the jobless recovery, it has become, ironically, its most prominent new victim. Even Chief Information Officer (CIO) jobs are in jeopardy.

As IT powers the brain-drain shift, IT employment itself leads the way to white-collar oblivion. A Gartner Inc. study predicts that 5% of all U.S. IT jobs will be moved offshore by the end of 2004. The rate is twice that for software-development and IT service-provider jobs: 10%.

Four currents are sweeping IT jobs, up to CIO, overseas or away entirely:

- **Continuing mergers and restructuring** that are combining multiple programmer, analyst or CIO positions into one.
- **Improvements by enterprise software and platform providers** that simplify installation, operation and maintenance. Translation: smaller IT staffs required.
- **Jobbing out of IT functions to service providers.** This not only reduces in-company IT staffs but overall IT employment, since service providers introduce economies of scale

97

to remain competitive. One of these economies is offshoring of the IT work, expected to siphon off 10% of U.S. IT service firm jobs by the end of 2004 according to Gartner Inc.

- **Emerging technologies such as Web Services** that are making systems more automatic and could turn computing into an external utility like electricity.

IT people seem to be shooting themselves in the foot as well as blasting employment in all fields facilitated by IT. It's not their fault, but that of myopia at the highest corporate, investment, and governmental levels. Still, the damage is being done.

The current job impact in IT should be viewed as a bellwether for other white-collar occupations. Any work that is location independent -- doable by phone or PC -- is endangered. If the work is largely culture-independent, like IT, it is especially vulnerable. It can be done by anyone anywhere on the globe who has English as a second or first language, and is willing to bone up on American ways.

Employment beyond IT, in IT-enabled fields, is following IT's job-loss lead. A survey by management consulting firm A.T. Kearney shows that financial-service firms such as banks, brokerages, and insurance firms will move more than 500,000 jobs overseas within five years.

Large business research and consulting firms including Forrester are promoting offshoring for its money-saving potential. For example, a 2003 white paper from Deloitte Consulting points to successes of off-shoring pioneer such as Citigroup and GE Capital, and advises clients that "lately offshoring has begun to undergo an important metamorphosis, transitioning from 'something to consider' to 'something that must be done.'" IBM, long resisting offshoring, is now joining the herd.

Job Creation not Automatic

"When technology eliminates jobs, it creates new, better ones." This old saw has been largely true until now. Technology did replace blue-collar jobs with new white-collar positions. But the future does not always mimic the past.

New employment is being created, but it's not always a step up from the disappearing kind. For example, during the last ten years, 1.7 million new jobs were created in the nation's eating and dining places, an increase of 26%. That's great if, when you lose your publishing or information technology job, you want to wait tables in TGI Friday's or cook fries in McDonald's. (Bear in mind, too, that if e-tech can create automated grocery checking, it can create automated burger serving and other new self-service options. Already, fast-food restaurants have streamlined food preparation and conditioned customers to fetch their own tableware, napkins and drinks.)

Small businesses have traditionally produced two-thirds to three-quarters of all the new jobs in America. Their ability to do so now is undermined by the flow of white-collar as well as manufacturing work abroad. Many small new white-collar businesses depend on sub-contracting that trickles down from the corporate giants. Much of that sub-contracted work is expected to flow to small suppliers near prime contractors abroad. In manufacturing, small U.S. suppliers of parts, materials, and maintenance are losing out too.

Ripple effects could be wide. For example, Ernst & Young predicts that offshoring will cut the demand for office space by 50 million square feet per year. With vacancy rates up, how will things go down for the nearby Starbucks or Staples? With a weakening of the intricate, interlinked business food chain, the small-business job engine could run out of gas. This could spell a long-term squeezing of the middle class.

Some economists believe there is a shift from working for others to working for oneself. However, entrepreneurship may not be our white knight. Many laid-off high-tech employees now bill themselves as "consultants" rather than admitting to being unemployed, seeking freelance projects while hoping for the job market to improve.

The reason that the old saw, "technology always creates new, better employment," doesn't ring as true today as it once did is that electronic technology is an entirely different animal. Work itself needs to be re-defined, and new forms of work need to be invented. This must happen intentionally, or the future will unfold chaotically, even tragically.

Workforce Turbulence?

A possible labor shortage due to retiring baby boomers -- cresting about 2020 -- could ameliorate the trauma of job loss and employment transition. However, the future is unpredictable:

- A workforce version of Moore's Law -- which states that microchip memory doubles in capacity every 18 to 24 months -- could obsolete human tasks much faster than we might imagine.
- Even if an acute labor shortage materializes, advancing technology will force continuing, possibly dramatic and accelerating adjustments in work relationships and functions.
- The increasing fluidity of information technology could fuel a homogenization of salaries globally -- with U.S. incomes falling to the level of rising Indian and Chinese pay.

One near certainty is that know-how tasks will follow the trajectories of farm and manufacturing tasks: increasing automation with the need for people to shift the focus of their contributions.

The likely course ahead -- the continued churning and challenging of the U. S. workforce -- does not bode well for America's middle class. We must intentionally make the future turn out profitably for all social sectors.

Positives and Negatives

A worldwide mental muscling-in is well underway and fast gaining momentum. Like machinery in the transition to the industrial age, electronic systems are potentially empowering us but currently displacing us. The benefits can be great but two drawbacks loom. They're the same drawbacks that prevailed as our muscles got augmented and replaced in the transition from the agricultural to the industrial age: (1) the trauma of transition, and (2) the prospect of unintended bad consequences at the mature end of the transition.

The present trauma of transition is likely to vex all of us and will severely oppress many. What are we supposed to do? What's the right career path for today's travel agent or VP of Information Technology? The infiltration of new technology is widespread and relentless. Safe, tsunami-free havens are becoming harder and harder to identify; white-collar, professional, and management people are being challenged even if their job type hasn't changed much, thanks to technology-driven restructuring that has morphed stable companies into volatile, short-term employers.

Unless we consciously intervene, the trauma of change, already acute for many, will challenge growing numbers as the transition to global electronic intelligence accelerates.

Greater Wealth & More Poverty?

The U.S. is commonly viewed as the world's richest nation, but our wealth is poorly distributed. The official U.S. poverty rate is 12.1%. That's 34.6 million poor and destitute Americans.

It's a dismal statistic compared to other free nations. According to the Organization for Economic Cooperation and Development (OECD), a greater percentage of Americans live below the poverty line than in 12 other leading nations including Canada, Germany, Japan, and Sweden. Our rate is about double France's and triple Finland's. Our poverty rate for children under 18 is double the rate of Western Europe; one in six of our future citizens grow up without means for adequate food, health care, housing, or higher education.

We seem to be growing into a high-tech banana republic with lots of wealth accumulated at the top, and lots of destitution at the bottom. According to the Luxembourg Income Study (2001), among 29 major nations, only Mexico and Russia have greater income disparity than America's.

Our middle class is hanging on, but just barely. According to Bureau of Labor Statistics data, during the "golden years" of American industry -- 1947 to 1973 -- real hourly wages grew by 75%. Since then they have stagnated. Consumer dept has reached record levels, and new bankruptcy filings by individuals totaled 1,573,720 for the 12-month period ending March 31, 2002, a new record, according to Administrative Office of the U.S. Courts.

Most Americans are working harder to maintain a stagnant lifestyle. According to the Economic Policy Institute, a two-parent family worked 16 more weeks per year in 2002 than in 1979. That's four extra months (two per parent), with additional costs for childcare, commuting, insurance, work clothes, and lunches.

Only the wealthy seem to be earning more. The Congressional Budget Office (CBO) reports mounting income disparity between 1979 and 2000. The poorest fifth of the population increased their after-tax income by less than 9%. The middle fifth, 15%. The top fifth, 68%. The top 1%, however, made 201% more. The disparity of wealth (total assets) is even greater. According to Federal Reserve data, by 1997 the top 1% of households had more savings, stocks, bonds, real estate and other assets than the bottom 95% combined.

Wealth accumulation is especially rampant among the CEOs of America's leading corporations, where employees are being shed and remaining workers squeezed through restructuring, factory closings, and offshoring. In Fortune's latest survey of the top 100 corporations, median CEO pay rose 14% from the previous year, in spite of huge losses for their stockholders, to $13.2 million.

Using OECD data, the Bureau of Labor Statistics reports that American CEOs make about twice as much as their counterparts in Belgium, Canada, France, Germany, Italy, Japan, Netherlands, Spain, Sweden, Switzerland, and the United Kingdom. The CEO of

MBNA Corporation, world's largest independent credit card issuer, netted $194.9 million in 2002. His firm charges consumers (some unemployed due to corporate cost-cutting) up to 27.98% interest when they miss payment deadlines on ballooning credit-card debt.

Surely there is no conspiracy. No organized group is intentionally transferring wealth from the nation's poor and middle class to the already rich. But significant transfer has taken place and shows no signs of abating. Motivated, most likely, by healthy self-interest run amuck, it is enabled by technology that allows more and more jobs to be performed anywhere, with or without the need for human involvement.

As American jobs flow overseas and into automation, the middle class could shrink and the unthinkable could happen: many white- as well as blue-collar families joining the ranks of the long-term unemployed and working poor.

However, technogreed, which co-opts the brain-drain trend to maximize money accumulation, threatens the wealthy along with everyone else. The recent recession destroyed trillions of stock-market wealth, most of it held by the top 10%. New upper-class pain could include:

- Failure to restore all of the recent large stock market losses of the wealthy, yet alone generate substantial new gains.
- Social backlash -- violent and cyber as well as activist -- that could challenge the current elite.

105

Pitfalls of Bad Planning

Myopically pursued, the end-state -- the mature information age -- could range from awful to barely tolerable, but even if it's miraculously wonderful, getting there could be rocky. Unmanaged transitions of this magnitude tend to dislocate the many while favoring the few. People get chewed up in changing gears. Who wants to be one of the grunts taking the brunt?

In addition, the future we find ourselves in, after years of transitional pain, might not be the cornucopia we hoped for. The mature information age could be mostly wonderful, but contain some rotten fruit. Depending on our actions now, we could flower into our best selves with plenty for all, or find ourselves trapped in a dying world.

If we fail to play our cards right, we could lose our mental dominance to electronic competence. Hello to our worst science-fiction nightmares.

Goodbye to our lucrative livelihoods, lush lifestyles, and eventually -- perhaps -- our very existence. But the electronic brain drain, properly managed, can take us to brighter destinations.

THE
SOLUTION

The problem is serious but fixable, and we can create a future as bright as the dangers are dark.

How?

5

Becoming Meta-conscious

Route to Better Jobs & Lives

To survive the brain-drain trend and create new wealth and a life for everyone, we need to elevate our aliveness. Why? Because the Earth has enough resources to support everyone in harmony, but only if we manage and multiply them right. That will take high intelligence and broad concern.

Our highest priority should be honing our creativity, productivity, responsibility, and other key aspects of our conscious behavior. Simultaneously, we need to tame our negative, suicidal qualities including technogreed, hatred, violence, discouragement, and passivity. We can do this while maintaining a healthy competition that does not transgress into destructiveness.

Survival depends on moving up from mind to metamind. We need to work on how we think, see, feel, relate to others, dream and achieve -- all aspects of our consciousness or aliveness. First we need to be clear about what human consciousness or aliveness is.

Twain Test vs. Turing Test

It is the year 2020 and Mark Twain graciously returns from the dead to help us answer a perplexing question: What does it mean to be alive?

In 2020 computers have started passing the Turing Test (devised in the 1900's by British mathematician Alan Turing). It's a simple way to find whether an artificially intelligent device really is thinking like a human. Testers ask questions of two entities behind two closed doors. One is a computer; the other, a real person serving as a control. If the testers can't tell the difference between the two, then the computer must be just as alive as the person.

Though many computers can now (in 2020) pass this test, most people remain unconvinced. When the smart devices are brought out into the open, somehow they just don't seem very human. They act smart, but there doesn't seem to be "anybody at home inside." Something is missing.

So a noted philosopher proposes a more subtle test: the Twain Test. If Mark Twain, history's savviest humanist, says a machine is alive, then it is, and not a moment before. The obvious problem with this test -- Twain's death in 1910 -- is overcome when a medium invokes the writer's spirit from the netherworld. Twain readily agrees to the task. He does not want any closed doors, though, and he dispenses with controls. "Just bring me the contraptions," he says. "If there's any whiff of human consciousness, I'll sniff it out."

All the computers that had passed the Turing Test promptly flunk the Twain Test, so the engineers go back to the drawing board. They bring the feisty spirit a series of more and more sophisticated devices based on neural networking, holographic memory, and quantum tunneling. "Not alive yet," says Twain over and over.

The engineers build in creativity, emotional response, sensitivity, and political correctness. All to no avail. "Not alive! ... Not alive!"

Then inspiration strikes. The engineers build in humor. Twain interviews a series of cyber comics, but never cracks a smile. "They tell a lot of jokes," he reports. "But they've got no delivery, and their material stinks." One day a comedic computer delivers a series of one-liners. Twain smiles in spite of himself, chuckles, and then roars with laughter. The engineers look at one another with satisfaction. At last!

But Twain punctures their balloon. He turns to them and says, "This gadget's OK. Really funny. It could go on tour. But alive? Nah."

The testing continues month after month, and Twain grows as frustrated as the engineers. He starts probing the devices with strange-sounding questions:

"What is your opinion of the color blue?"

"Is there anything you'd like to ask *me*?"

"When you consider existence versus non-existence, do you have any particular preference between the two?"

The answers only make Twain groan and droop with boredom. Everyone, including the great writer, feels like calling it quits.

Then one day an unpretentious, utilitarian computer is brought into the room -- the autopilot of an airliner that crashed. It's a plain black box with a robotic voice and few social graces. Twain eyes the device tentatively while the engineers stand in the background. "I understand you malfunctioned," he says to the flickering face of the black box. "When you were landing at O'Hare the other day. From what I hear, all that survived was the flight recorder and you." The black box remains silent.

"It was a pretty serious thing," continues Twain, puffing on his cigar. "I understand you could end up in a desk job, or maybe get sent to the scrap heap."

The black box flickers its lights nervously. "I hadn't heard that," it says.

"I have it on the highest authority," replies Twain.

Silence. The black box modulates its lights into a regular, nondescript pattern, "It wasn't my fault," it says. "It was the landing system."

"Aha!" exclaims Twain, jumping to his feet and turning to the engineers. "Signs of life at last. Prevarication. A human trait for sure. The ability to see what's clearly so and yet declare otherwise. Bald-faced lying to save one's own skin. Bending the truth in one's own selfish interests."

"But I wouldn't build too many of those things," he continues, pointing to the black box, tilting his head reflectively and blowing a smoke ring. "We've already got enough politicians."

If we're to create a future we care to live in, consciousness is our tool. But what exactly is that? Just how conscious are we today? And what are the chances for developing higher states of consciousness tomorrow? Let's start by examining the nature of our most human characteristic: bright, aware aliveness.

What Does It Mean to Be Alive?

Consciousness includes all our human qualities, emotional as well as rational, and more. If we equate consciousness with productive, rational processing of information, we miss the point. A truly conscious being not only computes but also knows; and not only knows but also makes choices. The knowing and the choosing make all the difference. Our unique consciousness includes creativity, emotion, and humor, but there's something more: an over-arching evaluation and determination of events. One name for it is "responsibility."

No computer has ever been convicted of a crime. Why not? Haven't they caused plenty of problems? Messed up records and siphoned off money? Sent airline passengers to their deaths?

We humans continue to be the only entities that can be found guilty. We're the responsible ones, the only responsible ones. But not all of us all the time. If you have a good lawyer, a jury might decide you were *non compos mentis*, Latin for "not having mastery of one's

113

mind." You're off the hook. Responsibility hinges on meta-consciousness. It's not enough to know that you did something. Awareness alone will not convict you. You've got to be aware *and* in control.

Being aware and in control is our core conscious strength. Let's understand that strength a little better. Where does the "in control" part come from?

QUESTION:

When you're asleep at night, are you responsible for your dreams?

Most people would say they bear no responsibility for their nocturnal reveries. Dreams just happen. One is carried helplessly along though the nightmare or sexual escapade. If you have lucid dreams, though, you might conclude otherwise. Lucid dreamers know they're dreaming while they're dreaming, and therefore gain the ability to control the dream's progress. Responsibility starts to apply. You could kill someone in a lucid dream and then convict yourself in your own mind.

Responsibility, the knowledge of right and wrong, love, and the ability to choose -- these are the qualities that make us special. They're functions of meta-consciousness, of reflection or the prescient, powerful awareness of awareness. *Meta*, coming from the Greek, means "beyond" or "transcending." Metamind is mind beyond mind; mind transcending and encompassing mind at a higher level. (In the rest of this book, I'll be

114

using several terms interchangeably: metamind, meta-consciousness, consciousness, awareness, aliveness, self-awareness, self-consciousness, reflection.)

So, what's the point? What's the value of being clear about what aliveness is?

Mentality Appropriate for the Information Age

As electronic systems take over more and more of our mental functions, we have the opportunity and the imperative to get stronger where we're already strong. It's time to develop and maximize our uniqueness, and consciousness is it. Our strategy for surviving the trauma of change is to develop our conscious qualities ranging from aware perception to wise decision making to unbounded responsibility. Our desired end state is a world enriched by high levels of meta-consciousness.

So what's our starting point? What's the current status of our minds? Just how conscious are we? And where should we go with it to negotiate the information age? Let's start by taking a closer look at the phenomenon of reflective consciousness.

The Wellspring of Human Power

The mature mind is more than plain awareness; it can do more than observe life's movie show. It can also direct the action. It can create, choose, and make things happen. The human mind, as it matures, gains the power to shape reality. But how? Our active power doesn't come from plain consciousness. It comes from consciousness of consciousness -- mind re-amplified, consciousness squared. It comes from reflection or the mind holding up a mirror to itself. That's the state where intentional behavior thrives.

This higher form of consciousness lifts us out of ourselves so we can look down and see alternatives. Reflective consciousness lets us do more than watch a bird fly; it lets us make a balloon that soars. This higher awareness is the thing that confers our magic powers of intention and creation. One might think that plain consciousness is enough to do the trick, but it isn't.

I think about thinking,
therefore I am.

With apologies to René Descartes

Being aware and aware of that fact is the thing that makes you "compos mentis" or in control. But it's not an all-or-nothing state.

In any given person, reflective consciousness turns on and off sporadically, like a light with a faulty connection. It varies by degrees. The more conscious of consciousness you are, the more alive and effective you are; the less meta-conscious, the more dim and robotic.

Reflection happens naturally as a matter of course; but it seldom happens thoroughly well and often, even in Nobel Prize-winning scientists. In biological and cultural evolution, reflective consciousness is a new phenomenon. It's still a novelty. Furthermore, it's less a part of our physiology than of our culture and education. Like the ability to play the violin, higher consciousness must be developed; we have to work at it. We're only now starting to get the knack of using it consistently and well.

It's Like a Special Form of Dreaming

The present state of consciousness can be better understood by comparing it to lucid dreaming. While you are asleep and immersed in a dream, it may dawn on you that you're dreaming, and -- while still as deep in slumber as ever -- you may start moving through the dream with a new overlay of awareness.

That's the lucid-dreaming state (well documented by Stephen LaBerge of Stanford University's Pshcyo-physiology Laboratory, and Patricia Garfield, co-

117

founder and past president of The Association for the Study of Dreams).

During one of my own lucid dreams, I found myself within a cathedral-like dome decorated with intricate, multicolored geometric designs. While moving within the dome as a kind of disembodied consciousness, I intentionally studied the rich variety of shapes and patterns; and as I did, I simultaneously marveled at the mind's ability to construct such a vision. Further, I began probing the mystery of my experience. Still deep in sleep and fully engaged in the dream's reality, I reflected that I had never seen such a cathedral ceiling. Where did the images come from, I wondered. Then I woke up.

The significant thing about lucid dreaming is this. The overlay makes a big difference in your experience. If the dream's a pleasant one, the pleasure is more consciously experienced. If the dream's a nightmare, the fear and horror are moderated, and the purgative value may be enhanced. Some lucid dreamers even analyze their dreams while dreaming them, I did in my cathedral-ceiling dream. But the overlay of reflective consciousness makes yet another difference.

Suddenly, since you know you're dreaming, you gain the power to influence the progress of your dream. If you choose, you can explore interesting byways, experience forbidden pleasures, probe deep-seated fears, invite impossible fantasies, solve real-world problems, and invite unexpected delights or insights.

Sporadic Reflective Consciousness

Lucid dreaming is, in fact, a form of reflective consciousness. Historically, our development of dream-state consciousness of consciousness seems to have lagged behind the emergence of waking-state consciousness of consciousness. So examining our bedtime consciousness can give us insights into the genesis and status of our daytime consciousness. Like the lucidity that is added to ordinary dreaming, the mind's daytime overlay of self-awareness conveys new color, pleasure, depth, and control.

You see real cathedrals or forests or people with new wonder, depth, and appreciation.

Lucid dreaming usually doesn't last long; it pops on, and then soon disappears. Waking-state reflective consciousness is also an on-off thing. Some people sustain it for relatively long periods. Others seldom experience it, living like automatons.

The quality of lucid dreams varies, too. Some people simply observe their dreams; others influence their dreams in trivial ways; some geniuses have used lucid dreams to achieve scientific or creative breakthroughs.

The quality of waking-state reflective consciousness similarly varies. You can be meta-conscious and yet add little value to your life. You can employ this higher consciousness to make some pretty good decisions and create some pretty good outcomes. Or, like Thomas Edison or Robert Goddard (inventor of the liquid-fuel rocket), you can use reflection to change the world. Most of us utilize only a fraction of our conscious potential.

A Society That's Often
Non Compos Mentis

Consciousness of consciousness enables responsibility. So if you want to find gaps in higher consciousness, look for shrugging shoulders and averted eyes, excuses and silence. As individuals we probably rate a C for responsibility. We do OK much of the time. And then there are those laws we seem to forget about, the overeating that seems to happen all by itself, the pain of others we somehow fail to feel.

Sometimes the unconsciousness is palpable. Anger flares or panic pierces; a knife lashes out; blood flows. Later the assailant remembers the event but says, "I didn't mean to; it just happened." It might be a lie; it could be true. We're all un-meta-conscious in many ways much of every day.

As a society we probably rate a D for responsibility. Somehow our individual reflective consciousness seems to dim as we gather in groups. In a small town, we might help someone who had a problem with their car. In New York City, it might be someone else's responsibility. Too often in our institutions the levels of consciousness and responsibility sink depressingly low. It's so easy to shrug and redirect, shuffle and avert, not see or hear, insulate oneself. Then when metaphorical blood flows, there's a better excuse than "I didn't mean to; it just happened." It's "I had nothing to do with it."

That's the problem with our social mind. The "I" gets lost. Both individual and group higher consciousness go to sleep.

Sometimes when people gather together in our society, meta-consciousness does not fade; it brightens, particularly in emotional and visceral dimensions. That's the attraction of live concerts and sporting events. And now and then in our businesses and governmental bodies, a magic thing happens. Rare individuals open their eyes and open their hearts, raise their hands and raise their voices. It's the rise of leadership that rouses our common consciousness.

Raising Consciousness

Although the quality of our individual and social consciousness may be less than stellar, the prospects for improvement are great. The quality of consciousness can be affected by an under-appreciated aspect of it: the ability to enhance itself. Just as reflective consciousness can be applied to improving outside reality, meta-consciousness can be turned inward to improve the working of the mind itself. When the active power of self-awareness focuses on the mind, and relevant processes are intentionally invoked, the mind grows increasingly powerful.

This has been demonstrated over and over again. For example, in a series of training sessions for corporate managers, I posed a question to participants. I asked them to imagine that they were in charge of the manufacture of the punched-hole data processing cards that fed data into early computers. The corners of the cards became frayed after repeated use, causing jams in the read-in devices.

I asked the managers to focus on this problem and come up with solutions. Invariably, they developed five to ten workable solutions within less than half an hour: making the cards out of fray-resistant plastic, adjusting the machines to detect frayed corners and shut down before damage is done; manufacturing the cards with rounded rather than square corners; and so on. In the 1960's, IBM in fact implemented a solution: round-cornered cards.

The point of the training sessions was this: It took IBM and the whole data processing industry 75 years to come up with a solution, while the groups of managers came up with workable solutions in minutes. The difference? Immediate, targeted application of reflective consciousness.

If you intentionally focus your mind on an issue, rather than waiting for "nature to take its course," you can achieve wonders. For those willing and able to self-direct their consciousness, things can happen now rather than 10 or 75 years from now. The key is focusing one's mind on focusing one's mind.

Without reflective consciousness, things stay as they are -- card-jamming problems persist forever. With reflective consciousness (natural, unprovoked meta-consciousness), things can be changed, though it may take 75 years. With frequent, self-induced reflective consciousness, things can be changed right away; or at least the seeds of change can be sown immediately.

That's good news for our prospects of easing the transition to the information age and creating the future we want. The more conscious you are, the more responsible and powerful you can be. For example, if you're highly conscious and your job is replaced by electronic intelligence, there can be a place for you on higher ground. The trick is to elevate one's consciousness. That calls for training.

Resources for Improvement

We now have the knowledge to help ourselves become more conscious in practical, fulfilling ways. Methods exist to help us tinker with the very workings of our mentality so we can intentionally call our active powers into play. The result can be mental gears milled and lubricated, humming more and more smoothly; minds that are self-inspected, reorganized and empowered.

There's a scarcity of good training materials, though: books, simulations, mind-building games, and electronic aids. In schools, universities, businesses, and non-business organizations, such tools are needed to help us get up to speed mentally, so we can more frequently monitor and fine-tune our processes of thought, perception and feeling to maximize our imagination, creativity, responsibility, and control.

We also need substantial new materials for developing all the specific meta-conscious skills that set us apart.

WHAT MENTAL TASKS ARE WE BETTER AT?

Humans excel at ...	E-systems excel at ...
METAMIND **MICRO SKILLS** 1. Basic thinking skills and symbolism. **MACRO SKILLS** 2. Conscious monitoring and control (perceptual and motor). 3. Hypothesizing. 4. Creativity and imagination. 5. Subjective decision making. 6. Social skills. 7. Responsibility (valuing, love, and pursuit of ethical objectives).	**DEFINED OPERATIONS** • Number crunching and routine logic. • Mass storage and retrieval. • Remote sensing and control. • Structured or routine decision making. • Control of repetitive processes. • Simple or labor-intensive instruction.

Let's zoom in a bit on our meta-conscious components. What exactly are they, and what's the value of enhancing them? Let's look first at our micro skills.

1. Basic Thinking Skills & Symbolism

The basic processes or micro elements of thought may be broken down into six types. These correspond to elements in the world, for we interact with reality only through the mind's window. The six elemental processes are:

- **Thing making or reification** (we notice an apple, say).
- **Qualification** (the apple is red).
- **Classification** (the apple is a fruit).
- **Structure analysis** (the apple has skin, seeds, pulp).
- **Operation analysis** (the apple grew and will be eaten).
- **Analogy** (your child is the apple of your eye).

An awareness trilogy -- sensation, emotion, and logic -- plays a role within each of these six elements.

- **Sensation** (we see, hear, and touch).
- **Emotion** (we feel angry, afraid, jealous, happy).
- **Logic** (we notice relationships of size, number, order, and causation).

To employ the six elemental processes and the awareness trilogy, we utilize symbols. For example, words like *apple, red, seed,* and *before;* and numbers as well as diagrams and scientific notation.

The key way to raise our consciousness with regard to symbols is to become more aware of their basic characteristic, ambiguity. That is, any symbol can mean a number of different things and shift meaning with ease. For example, *apple* can refer to a piece of the fruit, an entire apple tree, the flesh of the fruit (minus seeds and stem), the flavor which might be imparted to a cookie or soft drink, and so on.

Unconsciously for the most part, our minds pursue the six elemental processes, the awareness trilogy, and symbolism.

If we want to become hyper-human, we need to become more aware of these "atomic-level" mental processes and intentionally invoke them from time to time. In particular, we need to pay more attention to neglected areas of our aliveness, such as our emotions -- currently so severely repressed we scarcely realize there's a problem.

Our other hyper-human skills -- the macro skills, from creativity to responsibility -- all owe their existence to our micro-level or "atomic" mentality, just as organisms own their existence to atoms. These macro-level skills include conscious monitoring and control, hypothesizing, creativity and imagination, subjective decision making, social skills, and responsibility.

2. Conscious Monitoring & Control

We keep our eyes and ears open so we're alert to what's happening, particularly problems and opportunities. Then, when appropriate, we use our hands or speech to intercede -- prevent a mishap, seize an opportunity, or make an adjustment.

For example, let's say you grow apples and you're looking for ways to increase your income. You keep alert, constantly observing and thinking. One day, you notice a child eating candy-coated popcorn. Hmmm. Suppose the candy apple had not yet been invented. On the spot you visualize a candy-coated apple, and you're off on a new line of business. As you develop the business, you of course keep on with your conscious monitoring. For example, you watch your pots of caramel candy and turn down the heat before they boil over. Or you notice in the newspaper that there's going to be a craft fair in town; you ask a co-worker to set up a stand to sell your candy apples there.

Perception comes naturally; so do speech and the use of our hands. But skill at monitoring and control varies widely. The better we get at it, the more we make the world correspond to our desires.

3. Hypothesizing

As with creativity, hypothesizing involves a mental leap, but the leap is toward what already exists rather than what's new. When we're hypothesizing, we're looking for an explanation for a problem, for a state of affairs, or for a condition of nature.

For example, Newton asked why apples fell to the ground as they did, and came up with the theory of gravity. In your candy-apple venture, you might similarly look for explanations: "My candy apples aren't selling as well as they did last summer. How come? ... Is there a new competitor I don't know about? Have customer tastes changed? Is it the weather? Is there a problem with the packaging? Or what?"

The better we investigate, perceive, and analyze, the surer we are to find out what's going on and make the right conclusions or adjustments. In science and engineering, the better we analyze, the more knowledge we gain and the more power we give to society.

4. Creativity & Imagination

We invent new things in our minds. Then we may let them remain fantasies, or fashion them in reality like the Wright brothers constructing the first airplane.

Your original aha, visualizing a candy-coated apple, was of course an exercise of creativity. (It happened to employ the basic thinking skill of analogy: candy coating is to popcorn as candy coating is to apple.) You also employ creativity throughout the evolution of your business, dreaming up new options, possibilities, variations, and solutions. For example, suppose the reason your candy-apple sales are down is that a nearby apple grower has also gone into the business. Putting on your creativity hat you might develop a variety of candy-apple flavors: chocolate mint, coffee vanilla, etc. Do you also grow strawberries? Maybe you could dip them in caramel or chocolate.

The more attention we give to fashioning new possibilities, the more impact we have on our incomes, lives, and all aspects of evolving reality.

5. Subjective Decision Making

After using creativity to develop two or more possibilities, we clarify what we're after and then choose one of the possibilities.

For example, suppose you had not yet come up with the candy-apple business and were considering alternative ways of marketing your apple crop. "I want to make the most money ... I could sell the apples as they are, make them into apple sauce and then sell that, or make them into candy apples and then sell them in local stores.... Which is the way to go?" Later you would also of course use decision-making to determine which new flavors of candy apple to introduce, or which marketing avenues to explore.

The better we clarify what we're after and analyze the criteria of choice, the better we do in business and life.

6. Social Skills

We interact productively with other people and get them to interact productively with one another. Social skills include leadership, responding to leadership, motivating others, listening, speaking, reading body language, organizing, conveying a vision, and inspiring enthusiasm.

For example, you join a local service club to keep in touch. You learn from a fellow member that her church is looking for a good fundraiser. You figure a candy apple sale would be ideal, but you don't offer to sell your apples to the church. Instead, in a friendly way, you offer to donate 100 candy apples and to provide additional ones, if needed, at cost. You win appreciation for your generosity and also gain valuable public awareness for your product.

The more we hone our social skills, the more friends we make and the more positive activity we generate in others.

7. Responsibility

Responsibility is the crowning realization of integrated, well-functioning self-consciousness. In a state of responsibility, we're conscious and we know it. But there's more. Our awareness is maturely wide and includes other people as well as ourselves, ultimately all of humanity. Love and other values exist where there is responsibility, and we aim for goals that are ethical.

> For example, someone else in town starts to make and sell candy apples. You start dreaming up devious, not exactly legal plots for putting that person out of business, but catch yourself. Surviving in that manner isn't worth it, you figure. So you focus on ways to compete better by improving your product, service, and retail relationships.

The more we hone our responsibility, the better we feel about ourselves; and the healthier we make our community, industry, and society. Responsible behavior often sets us back temporarily, but offers the only path to our central goal: becoming more alive, connected, and powerful.

During earlier periods of history, it made sense to hone meta-consciousness. The best people did it, from Socrates to St. Paul, Leonardo to Ben Franklin. It makes particular sense now. Soon our lesser skills won't be needed. Electronic systems will supply the bulk of the --

- Facts and codified knowledge that we now retrieve from biological memory.
- Routine types of decision making, analysis, and number crunching such as we now perform with spreadsheets.

- Performance of tasks that call for observation and manipulation, such as driving a truck, assembling parts, operating a cash register, or drilling kids on Spanish.

Developing our hyper-human qualities has become our best career path, educational opportunity, and way to fulfill us as individuals -- not to mention an imperative for our survival. And it can to used to generate enormous new wealth (see chapter 10).

Mental Models to Make It Happen

In addition to profiting from metamind training, we can benefit from tools that remind us to use the skills as appropriate. Those reminder tools are "mental models." A mental model is any routine or entity that we call on over and over again to focus the active power of our minds. Here's a very simple but potent two-step model:

1. **Does it have to be this way?**
2. **How could it be different?**

Rewind twenty years and imagine yourself dragging a heavy suitcase along a sidewalk. "Does it have to be this way? ... How could it be different?"

"If only suitcases had wheels!" ... Of course, now they do, thanks to someone "popping up" into meta-mind by asking basic questions.

Our minds are the source of any and all control we have over our lives and the world; and this control comes on strong when we make ourselves knowingly consciousness through mental models. They help us pop up into a highly empowered, self-directed state. Here's a mental model often used by sales representatives:

1. **Approach**
2. **Interview**
3. **Propose**
4. **Handle objections**
5. **Close**

With this model, representatives check to see what stage they're in, and what stage they ought to be in to keep on track. For example, are they proposing Model X before they fully understand what the prospect's objectives are? Maybe Model Z would fit the bill better.

A few years ago I helped Pitney Bowes build such a model into a sales support system utilizing computers and daily planners.

Here's another mental model. I developed it after years of working on human and technical issues for IBM, AT&T, Cisco, and other leading companies.

DARE

It's an acronym for **Dream, Act**, and **React** within a state of **Enthusiasm**. The details, which I won't go into here, extend deeply into creativity, decision making, planning, mustering the courage to act, focusing on problems and getting at their causes, and maintaining the emotional control required for responsibility, effectiveness, and personal fulfillment.

Mental models help us intentionally "pop" ourselves up into higher consciousness more often and more appropriately than we would "naturally." Once their use becomes second nature, they can forever change the way we live our lives and perform our jobs.

Mind-extension software, discussed later in this book, can also help us leverage our metamind skills.

Lifting Society by Its Mental Bootstraps

Suppose -- in business, education, and all of society -- we were to launch a crash program to upgrade our conscious perception, emotionality, creativity, decision making, and human interaction including responsibility. What might the payoff be?

Aided by mental models, mind-extension software, and other means of strengthening meta-consciousness, we might --

- Become much more productive in our jobs, frequently obsoleting tasks to work higher on the metamind scale.
- Gain a better appreciation of what our minds are and what we ourselves can be within society and life.
- Increase our mastery of truth and falsehood as well as good and bad behavior.

- Enhance our daily experience through deeper experiences of sensory awareness, emotion, logic, creativity, and human connection.
- Participate more fully in various "group minds" and a possible emerging "global mind" (discussed later).
- Create unprecedented wealth through technological and social advances.
- Change the world by adding to the social responsibility that shapes all institutions and human interactions.

How Powerful Can We Get?

Consciousness, however well developed, has its limits. Unlike God, we may never be able to create something out of nothing. Try saying, "Let there by light" and see what happens. But our creativity has sometimes seemed almost godlike. Thomas Edison said in so many words, "Let there be a light bulb." And soon there was light -- a new kind of light -- all over the world.

Our present level of consciousness -- rating only a C or D -- may be puny compared to its potential. Yet it's not so shabby. Think of the world we might live in when we rate an A+.

How far might we go? Where might we end up? Ask yourself, what do you want? Down deep? All of us want something, yearn for something. What?

Ultimately, it may simply be more life, more participation and connectedness, more creation.

An expanding mind is both our destination and our vehicle. We have the opportunity to grow our mentalities and transform our surroundings as never before. Our future can be very bright; it may be brightness itself.

The brightness we seek will not be easy to achieve, however. We face one enormous hurdle in particular. It's the difficulty of bringing into line the most enlivening, delightful, and yet troublesome aspect of our consciousness: responsibility with its social breadth of consciousness including love. Responsibility and love, as we shall see, have a curious connection to death.

That connection is particularly evident right now, and it's a connection we need to adjust.

6

Overcoming Intentional Death

The Conscious Way to Save Our Skins

Directly and indirectly, suddenly and slowly, aided or goaded by technology ... people are killing people. It's our biggest problem. We've got to solve it or our species probably won't survive. First we need to understand it.

Suppose, during the year of the 9/11 tragedy, 2001, there were no murders in the United States, no military casualties, and the Attack on America never happened. Which of the following statements would be true?

- **The overall death rate would have been 4% less.**
- **There would still have been plenty of death by human hand.**

In 2001 about 2,405,000 Americans died. Murder claimed 16,137; the Attack on America claimed about 3,000; there were virtually no military casualties, but let's suppose there were 393, the number who died during the Gulf War under the first President Bush. The grand total is 19,530, less than 1% of the total deaths from all causes.

The first statement is way off the mark, but the second is right on. Why? Because death by human hand doesn't happen just through murder, terrorism, or war. Lots of Americans take their own lives. And that's only part of a larger problem.

Serious Self-destruction

The plain, sobering fact is that more of us do ourselves in than get killed by others. Suicide claimed 28,332 lives in 2001, 76% more than murder and 45% more than murder, military action, and terrorism combined.

Suicide usually happens through lack of a broad self-consciousness that includes other people. When we're self-conscious as "we," we tend to hang on no matter how tough the going gets. When we're self-conscious as "only me" -- all alone -- that's when we're at risk.

Self-inflicted death is a big problem. Since 1900, when America began tracking such things, the suicide rate has always exceeded the murder rate, usually by a wide margin. The same is true of most other countries. In Hungary, Finland and Switzerland, as many as ten or more people kill themselves for every person murdered.

In only a few countries, such as Mexico, has murder outpaced suicide.

On a dark street at night, the most dangerous thug one is likely to meet is oneself. But suicide is far from the only form of self-inflicted death, and it's far from the only lethal axe that falls on us for lack of a broad self-consciousness that embraces others.

QUESTION:

Suppose one motorist habitually talks on a cell phone while driving, and another habitually lights up cigarettes while driving. Which one takes the bigger risk?

- The talking motorist
- The smoking motorist

Serious Slow Slaughter

There were 41,821 traffic fatalities in the U.S. in 2001. No one knows how many may have been precipitated by inattention due to cell phone use or smoking; 16,653 of the deaths were alcohol-related. The odds of death by crash may be about equal for the talking and smoking motorists, though a driver with cell phone in hand may be more distracted. Smoking carries its own heavy hazard, however, claiming the lives of an estimated 430,000 Americans each year.

There are many slow, drawn-out forms of self-inflicted death: cigarette smoking, alcohol and drug abuse, inactivity, over-eating and junk food diets. Then there's careless driving and other accident-prone behavior.

The top four causes of death in 2001 were heart disease, cancer, stroke, and chronic lower respiratory disease. But what causes *them?* Many of the contributing factors are lifestyle choices under our control, such as the foods we eat and addictions we court. Nicotine is the main villain behind lung cancer, chronic bronchitis, emphysema, heart disease, and stroke. We rightly got up in arms when Al Queda killed more than 3,000 of us. When cigarettes kill many times that number, we hardly raise our eyebrows.

It would take 143 terrorist attacks of the magnitude of the one on the World Trade Center to equal the annual carnage of smoking. That's one attack every two and a half days, year after year.

The following chart puts some of the causes of death in perspective:

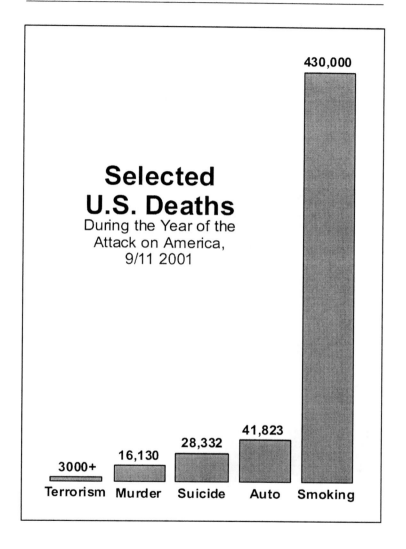

Selected U.S. Deaths
During the Year of the Attack on America, 9/11 2001

Category	Deaths
Terrorism	3000+
Murder	16,130
Suicide	28,332
Auto	41,823
Smoking	430,000

What's Going On Here?

Let's look more closely at how we're dying and may continue to die as the information age matures and technogreed endures. The types of death that should concern us most are the ones that involve conscious awareness and are triggered by human intention. They may be classified as follows:

INTENTIONAL DEATH (sudden)
- **Killing others** (murder, military & police action)
- **Killing self** (suicide)
- **Killing self and others** (terrorism or murder-suicide)

SEMI-INTENTIONAL DEATH (gradual)
- **Killing others** (pollution, tobacco industry, narcotics trade ...)
- **Killing self** (smoking, alcohol & drug abuse, over-eating, careless driving ...)
- **Killing self and others** (shared addictions, careless driving with passengers ...)

Death by human intent is either clearly intentional and sudden, or semi-intentional and slow or delayed. People who commit suicide know they're taking their own lives. Those who die of lung cancer kind of know what they're doing when they keep on puffing, but time seems forgiving and they put it out of mind.

Both types of death -- intentional and semi-intentional -- come in three flavors: killing of others, killing of oneself, and killing of oneself and others at the same time. Lack of broad, inclusive self-consciousness helps inspire all three types; ironically, the *presence* of inclusive self-consciousness provides large doses of motivation for the first and third types: killing of others, and killing of oneself and others at the same time. We will explore how in a moment. First let's examine the nature of the types.

The intentional killing of others is considered murder, terrorism, or lethal action by military personnel or police. The intentional killing of oneself is usually considered suicide. The intentional killing of oneself and others is considered terrorism or mayhem by a deranged individual.

The semi-intentional killing of others happens all the time and gets too little attention. It should probably be called slow murder. An outcome of technogreed, it happens when manufacturers knowingly pollute, and when cigarette makers and drug pushers do their thing.

The semi-intentional killing of oneself also gets too little attention. It might be called slow suicide. It happens when people indulge their indulgences with full knowledge of the risks, and when they knowingly increase the odds of accident (as, drinking and then driving). Some forms of slow suicide (such as cigarette smoking and cocaine use) might be called slow assisted suicide, since outside "pushers" help push death nearer.

The semi-intentional killing of self and others is akin to international terrorism but may be wholly domestic. Examples include abusing drugs while pressuring your friends to do the same, and drinking and then driving with others in the car.

143

Quantitatively, killing oneself (suicide and slow suicide) is a mountain of a problem; so is killing others when slow murder is figured in the total. Killing oneself and others at the same time (terrorism and shared addiction, etc.) is by comparison a molehill of a problem, though quite serious and with the potential to grow. All three types call for effective action from a new vantage point.

What's the Point?

We can't do much about lightning that strikes without warning, or truly accidental accidents. But when death happens on purpose or we know our actions increase its likelihood or speeds its arrival, we can act differently. (We can also, of course, combat "natural" forms of death such as cancer or pneumonia, but that's a topic for another book.) The big question is, just how can we change our behavior to combat the monumental problem is intentional death?

If conscious will is at the root of our destructive behavior, clearly we need to do something about consciousness, but what? Before addressing this question, let's explore intentional death a bit more.

Murder, by legal definition, is a conscious act by a responsible human; and most murder involves at least occasional conscious moments of consideration, decision making, and planning. Most people who kill are considered legally responsible for their acts, or "compos mentis" rather than "non compos mentis."

Death by intention involves higher consciousness by definition. We need to be aware and in control in order to do anything on purpose or to make choices based on information that is known to us. That includes murder, suicide, slow murder, slow suicide, and quick as well as slow forms of murder-suicide.

Consciousness is at the core of all intentional death. What does that tell us? It seems contrary to the proposition that the cultivation of higher consciousness may be our only good strategy for surviving the information age. Given its criminal record, should we let higher consciousness roam around free? Should we let it get stronger? The answer is a qualified yes.

One key form of higher consciousness is especially relevant to death by intention: self-consciousness that includes others -- the extended aliveness of "we," often called "love." It is the territory of responsibility. When experiences of "we-ness" overtake us, our consciousness brightens. We come more alive; we expand into a delightful state of connection. We experience ourselves as more than ourselves; the other person and we are momentarily "one" to some slight or great degree. And the other person and we may feel part of a larger supporting reality.

More "we-ness" or love, we might suppose, is the much-needed antidote to all the intentional death that plagues us. True, but only partially so. This shared or overlapping consciousness also kills.

Death as the Fruit of
Shared Consciousness

While intentional death happens for lack of inclusive meta-consciousness or love; it also happens because of it. Feeling alone, unloved, and worthless, a woman jumps in a lake and drowns. Another woman jumps in a lake to save a drowning child, knowing she may drown in the attempt. Let's say she does drown. We call the first act suicide; the second, sacrifice or heroism. What makes the difference? The intention and the presence or absence of love. Lack of love motivates the first death; love, the second.

The killing of oneself usually arises out of lack of shared consciousness or connectedness. The reverse is often true when we take the lives of others. Love or connectedness is frequently at the root of it. For example, soldiers in battle don't typically kill for lack of connection; it's not feeling alone and worthless that makes them shoot or bomb. Quite the opposite. They may kill in part because they hate the enemy, but hate pales in comparison to the prime motive. Soldiers kill because they love their families and the country they're protecting. Even more, they kill out of closeness to their comrades in battle; it's the common bond that empowers them to strike.

Why do police officers kill? Maybe a few sickos do it out of alienation or resentment, but not the vast majority. Most do it because it's their job and they care about the community and the people they're protecting.

Inclusive self-consciousness. Connection with those they serve and protect. Love.

What about murder? It may often be done out of malice, selfishness, desperation, alienation, or hate. Sometimes, as in organized crime, it's done out of protective instincts like those harbored by soldiers and police officers. Mafia organizations are "families" and killing may preserve "family values."

The same principle holds for slow murder. It's seldom motivated by lack of shared consciousness or connection.

Cigarette-company employees don't promote death on purpose; killing isn't their objective, though they're culpable. They don't have it in for people; and they don't assault lungs and hearts because they feel alone and worthless. They do it because they love their families and want to support them; they also care about their fellow workers and want to help everyone succeed. Many drug pushers aren't as evil or down-and-out as often portrayed. The drug trade can be a very good business; it supports the pushers and the people they care about.

Slow murderers are like air force pilots who kill from afar; they don't see the slaughter up close, so the damage they do may shrink from view. A World War II veteran I used to work with reports: "I didn't really know what I was doing until I made a raid at very low altitude. I could see the men jostling and talking in a personnel carrier below me. My bomb hit dead on. There was a gray cloud and I could see arms and legs flying about. I saw a head that shot up then arched over

147

and down. Then it hit me, and I felt sick to my stomach. I wasn't just bombing toy trucks and tanks and buildings. There were real people down there."

If cigarette makers and other slow murderers saw their victims' agony up close, they'd probably get sick to their stomachs too. But the carnage is all so distant.

The murder-suicide of terrorism may stem mostly from lack of love when terrorists are loners, but they seldom are. Love or extended self-consciousness comes into play when there's a supporting group, especially one that shares deeply held beliefs.

Love & Killing, Pride & Suicide

Religion addresses the emotional and spiritual sources of intentional death. In Christianity, for example, the highest virtue is love. The worst sin is pride. Not pride as self-worth, but pride in the sense of separation and a turning away from others and God. Love and pride occupy opposite ends of a continuum. Love is an opening up and joining together with others and universal spirit. Pride is a closing in and cutting off from others and from the spiritual base that makes life vital and worthwhile.

Suicide and slow suicide stem mostly from pride or isolation. Murder and slow murder stem in large part from love. So does group-supported murder-suicide. But neither murder nor murder-suicide stems from love at the top at its continuum. These acts stem from love lower down, a form of love that religion warns against.

When Love or Extended
Self-consciousness Is Limited

When love and pride combine, somewhere in the middle of the continuum, we get a qualified kind of love -- love with limits, love that joins but also separates. Religion in its purer forms preaches love without limits: unqualified love, unbounded love.

But few of us practice the principle well, so in the real world love has boundaries. Sometimes love is very narrow, sometimes very wide; but it almost always has limits. Death happens beyond the limits. In the Mafia, love may extend no farther than the width of a particular "family." In a country such as China or Canada, love may end at the national borders. In a company that pollutes or sells junk food, love may extend no farther than one's family and fellow workers.

Limited-width love or meta-consciousness is like ethnic and sexist humor that is simultaneously funny and mean. It's warm and good within its limits but destructive beyond.

People love in all kinds of limited widths: the width of one's family, professional group, economic class, race, ethnic background, school, geographic region, etc. The range of our love may be limited to those who share our level of intelligence, our profession or specialty, our disability, or our multilevel marketing downline.

People who fit within one's range are the ones who really count. Others don't matter much; in fact, if they threaten the narrow group, they're the enemy.

149

Defensive action, even killing, may seem justified. Though hostile to blacks, KKK members have shared a lot of chumminess with one another.

Limited-width love or meta-consciousness has always been a big problem for humanity, justifying war, genocide, lynching, and enforced starvation. Even when motivated by religious values, it leads to no good. Whenever devout people love one another and it stops there, look out. Narrow Christian love gave us the bloody Crusades and Inquisition. The narrow love of Muslim extremists gives us much of today's terrorism.

Even those who say they "love everybody" often draw the line somewhere. They leave out all the human refuse that litters city streets. Or they include the homeless but exclude criminals. Or they include all criminals except murderers, rapists, or child molesters. Or they include everybody except evil terrorists.

Limited self-consciousness that extends to few others -- close-to-home love with a good dose of pride or self-separation mixed in -- may not appear to explain murder in all cases. It is often said that genocide by the likes of Hitler is motivated by the desire to dominate.

In 2002 the United Nations war crimes tribunal accused Slobodan Milosevic, the ousted Yugoslav leader, of crimes against humanity that led 200,000 people to their graves. What led him to do it? According to chief prosecutor Carla Del Ponte, it was basically the "search for power." That may be so, but the craving for power rises out of more basic motives -- the insecurity of self-separation commingled with limited consciousness of oneself and one's partners in crime.

These narrow, cozy motives get the bloody process started; mindless habit and the momentum of the game keep it going.

The challenge offered by religion and sense is to move up from pride to broader and broader love or inclusive self-consciousness. Human survival may require shared consciousness as wide as the planet.

Metamind Over Megadeath

As a practical matter, given who we are and where we are, just *how* can we broaden our inclusive awareness and thereby rise above intentional death?

Unlimited meta-consciousness does not require us to condone harmful actions of others. It does not prevent us from protecting ourselves or even taking life when there's no other alternative. It does not mean we need to embrace the sickness, stupidity, or evil intent of others. It does not mean we have to stop getting mad at people who cut us off in traffic or crowd ahead of us in line. It does not require us to cozy up to everyone.

It *does* require us to stop considering some people inherently evil, expendable, worthless, or irrelevant.

The world is full of nasty people bent on depriving us of our money, possessions, opportunities, freedoms, health, and lives. Some act out of economic desperation. Others wear expensive suits, live in multiple mansions, and do their dirty work behind the shield of the law. It would be too much to ask of us, as mere humans, to love these people. A more

151

reasonable objective is to shield ourselves from them without becoming like them. A longer-term objective is to fix our social systems so fewer of our children choose the dark side.

Overcoming intentional death is no easy task. It involves much more than changing the way we feel about others. It involves cultivating mature skills of responsibility. For example, suppose you work as a guard in a prison. One day when the warden is gone a fire breaks out and the alarm does not sound because the power is out. The warden would normally handle such a situation.

What will you do? You'd be smart to save your skin; get out of there quick. But your mind "pops up" to a higher awareness and concern. "I'd better warn my buddies."

The breadth of your shared consciousness or responsibility is widened. But then you think, "Maybe I can save all the guards," and you start organizing your buddies to spread the word and alert the fire department.

Your common consciousness has widened further, but how about the prisoners? Maybe you could save them too, all except for the murderers on death row.... "Okay, I'd better save them too."

Your consciousness, your breadth and level of responsibility, has broadened considerably. Has it reached its limit?

You think a bit higher and broader, including people in the surrounding community. If you save all of the prisoners including rapists and child molesters, some of them could get loose and do harm. "How can I save them and maintain security at the same time?"

Responsibility is a very high and wide capacity, a hard-won art that requires practice, gradual development, and the marshalling of multiple human skills including creativity, decision making, action, monitoring and control. Caring, of course, is a vital part of the mix but far from sufficient.

Many of our leaders today act like the prison guard a few levels below the "top" one in this example. Take care of my buddies in the merger but let everybody else fend for themselves. The community, the country? Not my responsibility.

Cultivating High-quality Metamind

While very broad common consciousness is required to magnify responsibility and overcome intentional death, it must be of the right type. Lower levels of quality are far less effective, even destructive.

Terms like *self-consciousness* and *reflection* suggest an overly logical, pale view of our unique mental state. Metamind is much more than knowledge, reason, understanding, or perspective. It is much more than dispassionate forms of responsibility. It is rich in emotion. The prevailing emotion of any moment of consciousness, however, can be thoroughly positive or negative in a variety of flavors.

The emotional atmosphere of metamind may take one of four forms. Only the first is thoroughly good and effective in foiling intentional death.

Atmosphere 1: Enthusiasm, energy, euphoria. This is spirit at its best, though I shy away from the term *spirit* because of its religious baggage. In this pure, pristine form of metamind, one lives within an aura of energy and excitement, even ecstasy sometimes. The prevailing feelings are joy, happiness, delight, and love.

This pleasant condition is highly practical and socially beneficent, the only sure route to the widest span of inclusive consciousness and responsibility. It is the state of flow or full, unimpeded aliveness. It is the atmosphere in which creativity flourishes, and the aha's of discovery emerge. It's the aura in which people work and live harmoniously. We need to "pop up" into this emotional stratosphere, at least for a microsecond, in order to have any new idea, learn any new concept, or reach any meaningful accord.

Atmosphere 2: Trying or efforting. Here we have good intentions but our aliveness has dimmed. The fun goes out of work; activity proceeds robotically. Time drags or there's not enough of it. Winning becomes our only hope because the present has lost its savor. Security and acquisition become paramount. A focus on possible loss and potential gain kill the kicks of now.

In this mental state we're more likely to take than create, more prone to compete than cooperate. The conviction of "not enough for all" is reinforced because we in fact don't have "enough" (satisfaction, that is) right now. Negative feelings -- notably fear, resentment, and greed -- prevail.

This mental atmosphere is the driving force behind technogreed. Though the least worst of the three unsatisfactory atmospheres, it is the likeliest to terminate the planet. Why? Because it supports virtuous notions of self-preservation that justify counterproductive efforts to suppress the two worst atmospheres. The means it employs include cutthroat business practices, economic genocide (globally and within the U.S.), knowing pollution, and war.

Atmosphere 3: **Addictive escape or avoidance.** As in atmosphere 2, the "now" is unsatisfactory, but we postpone trying to make tomorrow better. Our desires seem too distant and hard to attain. So we seek relief in present-moment indulgences that are counterproductive substitutes for the wholesome joy of atmosphere 1.

Our escapist indulgences include the usual suspects: overeating, smoking, excessive drinking, and drugs. They also include subtler escapes such as daydreaming as a substitute for action, driving too much or too fast, gossiping, watching too much mediocre TV, reading too much second-rate literature, and shopping for the sake of shopping.

Atmosphere 3 is characterized by guilt (ignored but nagging in the background), repressed feelings of fear and anger, discouragement, and mixtures of hopelessness and vain hope.

We tolerate most addictive escape because "it's only human" and everyone does it. Yet it contributes materially to intentional death, indirectly and often directly. It makes us weaker and detracts us from activity that could make life better. Through its withdrawal, it tacitly condones other people's brutish behavior stemming from atmosphere 2.

Atmosphere 4: Killing. Here we literally kill -- ourselves and/or others. We sink to this low atmosphere when the behaviors of atmosphere 2 or 3 get really bad.

In the trying mode we get to a point where the world or an opponent seems bent on our destruction. We fall from the trying to the killing mode. Now it's them or us; so we resort to the gun or bomb. We have no choice, it seems.

In the addictive mode, when our indulgence sinks beyond the point of self-control, we fall into the killing mode. Our moderate self-destruction becomes lethal with a vengeance. Drug addiction, drinking, smoking, or overeating may progress to a point of no return. Early death, though slow in coming, becomes almost inevitable.

Atmosphere 4 is characterized by repressed negative feelings of all types including sorrow, fear, and anger. Resentment may be acute; discouragement and hopelessness, profound.

Atmosphere 4 comes on gradually and then suddenly it controls us. Falling to the low regions of atmosphere 2 or 3, we pass a threshold where death starts to seem the only answer. So we deal death --

quickly or slowly, to ourselves or to others, or to ourselves and others at the same time.

Then people in atmosphere 2 often step in with self-righteous interventions. Their aim is to fight the destructiveness of atmosphere 4. But their efforts usually work only marginally or backfire. Only the fully positive force of atmosphere 1 can effectively counter the negativity of the other atmospheres.

One must somehow bring oneself and others up to that level. This can be tricky, though. If you're at a lower level at the time, you may sound hypocritical and fake. If you *are* at the top level, you'll have little difficulty bringing others up too. Your spirit alone may be sufficient without the need to say anything.

The four emotional atmospheres are encompassed by the DARE mental model mentioned in the previous chapter.

Metamind in its high, pure form will become easier to reach when we focus more attention on managing our emotions. "Managing" may sound like controlling, but good emotional management involves *expressing* emotions, not bottling them up.

Expressing emotions isn't just communicating them. A sense of the word *express* is "to remove," as in "express the oil from olives." The key idea of emotional expression is not just to let others know how we feel, but to get rid of the bad stuff that's in us.

Expression Over Repression

If we want to be our best selves and avoid annihilation through intentional death, it's imperative to purge negative feelings -- to get them out of us so good, productive feelings can reemerge (atmosphere 1).

Doing that isn't easy, because we've got a big problem with emotions today. Expressing how we feel is socially risky in most settings most of the time. Humor (an antidote to fear, anger, resentment, and other negative feelings) is the one outlet thoroughly approved for public consumption, and we owe a great debt to all our comics and friends with a light touch.

Social signals induce us to suppress most of the feelings we might express through other possible avenues.

Sorrow (expressed through tears) is seen as out of place at work, in public venues such as shopping malls and playing fields, in classrooms, and even in millions of homes -- especially when the tears are male. Anger (expressed by loud talking, shouting, and violent-seeming but harmless motion) enjoys few outlets. Action movies and sporting events offer the most widespread acceptable occasions for purging anger; but the effects are usually vicarious and incomplete. Fear (expressed through trembling and talking) is definitely something we're supposed to bottle up. "Get a grip."

There's nothing wrong, of course, with postponing emotional expression so long as the feelings get expressed sometime relatively soon. Today, however, suppression has become chronic and we're suffering the behavioral consequences. Millions of Americans are like radiator systems with the steam valves removed. Everything is ok … ok … ok … and then suddenly, BAM! The boiler blows.

A common characteristic of our homegrown terrorists is their passivity, up to a point. "He seemed like such a quiet boy." Suppress … suppress … suppress … and then suddenly, BAM! Columbine.

The lack of adequate emotional expression hurts us more deeply and in more ways that we may imagine. For example, war news and tough political stances have become emotional expression replacements like football and boxing. "Give it to 'em!" For the sake of a marginal purging of long repressed anger, resentment, fear, and discouragement, we tacitly condone lethal practices that threaten us all.

We need to re-examine our society-wide repression and start managing our emotions better. Our future requires mature, robust metamind of the highest type, with all its steam valves working.

Life & Death Ahead

To survive the transition to the mature information age and create a desirable future, we need to reverse the present trends of narrow responsibility and emotionless, spiritless mentality that contribute to intentional death. Without assertive, very conscious action, the trends could get worse.

In summary, our greatest dangers (in order of magnitude) seem to be --

1. **Suicide and slow suicide,** due to pride or self-separation.
2. **Killing and slow killing,** due in large part to narrow responsibility, consciousness, or love.
3. **Sudden and slow forms of murder-suicide,** also due in part to narrow forms of inclusive consciousness.

All forms arise from lower levels of metamind that flourish through lack of emotional expression. All forms are lethal and could spiral out of control. The forms are not, however, separate but intertwined. They feed on one another and make the total carnage worse.

Consider substance abuse. According to the U. S. Department of Health and Human Services, annual deaths due to alcohol abuse have soared to more than 100,000 recently -- more than murder, suicide and terrorism combined. Deaths attributable to drug addiction have increased to more than 38,000. When the 430,000-plus tobacco-related deaths are added to the grand total, substance abuse accounts for 25% of all American deaths.

The assisted-suicide of substance abuse extends beyond its own carnage, however. It also causes death elsewhere. Drinking accelerates death by auto accident. The drug trade and drug addiction instigate crime of all sorts, including murder.

Drug-related crime has been decreasing in American cities but increasing in small towns. Officials speculate that pushers have simply left urban areas for greener pastures; there are easy pickings out in the sticks, and law enforcement is less well funded there (due to loss of income from farming and manufacturing). In some small towns, murder rates have increased several times over, with most if not all of the killing drug-related.

The slow assisted suicide of substance abuse costs America an estimated $400 billion a year. That includes direct medical costs, losses in productivity, loss of future earnings when people die young, and costs of running social-welfare programs and beefing up law enforcement. This drag on society extends ever outward in subtle ways. It increases the burden of taxes, slows economic growth, makes streets less safe and lives more risky, and piles stress on everyone. It's enough to make one light up a smoke or take a drink.

Our Greatest Danger

In terms of gross numbers and social impact, slow assisted suicide (the combination of slow suicide and slow murder) appears to be our greatest danger by far, with substance abuse leading the charge. Pride or self-separation, with all its discouragement and hopelessness, appears to trigger it -- but not without assistance. This assistance, amounting to slow murder, stems from narrow shared consciousness and goes hand in hand with technogreed. It is also fostered by the lower three mental/emotional atmospheres.

This causal pattern is especially easy to see with substance abuse. Drug pushers and employees in tobacco and alcohol industries give too little mind to the consequences of their marketing efforts; but they're not alone in their self-limited consciousness.

Employers in general give too little mind to the effects of their layoffs, restructurings, and financial finagling. And all of us seem to forget the cascading effects of some of our lifestyle choices and community actions or lack of them. For example, we shop at a big chain store to save a few bucks and forget about the small retailers we are putting out of business and the low wages we are helping to enforce.

In the 1990's drug pushers moved into Prentiss, Mississippi, as they did into many other small American communities. In 1999 the largest employer in town moved its factory to Mexico. The unemployment rate shot up to 25%. The use of crack, marijuana, methamphetamine, and OxyCotin skyrocketed. So did crime. The murder rate in the county zoomed to 50 per 100,000 -- eight and a half times the national rate. To a casual observer, there were positive signs as well: new-home construction and healthy business in local stores. But some of the nicer homes were inhabited by affluent pushers; and in the stores, it was illicit money that made cash registers ring. "Drugs have become our major industry," said county sheriff Henry McCullum, quoted in the New York Times. "Almost everyone living in this community is profiting from the escalating drugs, directly or indirectly."

In some degree, America today may be Prentiss writ large; the world may be Prentiss writ larger. So where might we be going?

Downhill Trend?

The motivations for intentional death may or may not be getting stronger. The means of inflicting death are becoming more plentiful and available, however. Thanks to advancing technology, the tools of destruction are everywhere:

- Addictive substances and health-destroying foods.
- Guns and explosives.
- Chemicals that pollute and poison.
- Code that can crash airplanes or disable hospital equipment.
- Modern transportation that gives wrongdoers the world as their playground.

Striving, addictive, and killing mindsets are being fostered by social forces fed by technogreed. Alienation is often the most noticeable symptom.

Consider the progressive pruning of the family from extended family to nuclear family to single parent household. Now the single-*person* household is gaining vogue. There's lots of opportunity for aloneness, separation, and worthlessness. Consider the undaunted decimation of the company as "work family." Lifetime employers have become layoff mills; and many companies have lost any pretense of corporate community through constant mergers, acquisitions, restructuring, and disappearing acts. Togetherness isn't exactly being nurtured, and self-worth is being challenged at every instance of sudden joblessness.

While suicide is the eighth-leading cause of death in the U.S. for all ages, it's the third-leading cause for young people between 15 and 24. Have information-age influences contributed to this? Will mounting high-tech influences contribute even more?

And how about the technogreed influences on slow suicide? Why do so many people keep on smoking even though the Surgeon General has painted the dangers so clearly? What will happen if information-age forces push alienation to new limits? Will more people inhale lethal doses of nicotine? Will more turn to alcohol, cocaine, Ecstasy, and rich desserts? Look at alcoholism in Russia; already off the charts.

Modern communication aids and abets slow murder (or slow assisted suicide). It helps the drug trade thrive in small towns like Prentiss. It also oils the machinery of the pushers of legal substance abuse. Modern communication also lets all pushers keep their distance, remote from the consequences of their actions.

All forms of intentional and semi-intentional death aren't exactly ameliorated by the stress of job loss, corporate instability, and chaotic change.

Reflect that today's core trend is the transference of mental functions into electronic systems. That's a very big deal. It could be much more destabilizing than the earlier transfer of physical functions into machines; at least the industrial age created new jobs requiring know-how. It's not clear that the information age will follow a path that leads to vital new roles for the majority of people. It's not clear that towns and cities will be made more cohesive rather than less so.

Unnecessary, rootless people aren't likely to have much self-esteem. If self-worth plummets and alienation escalates, we shouldn't be surprised if suicide moves up on the charts. Slow suicide, too. The bottle, the weed, the powder or the pill may offer comfort found nowhere else.

When people get threatened or displaced, some react outwardly instead of inwardly. We could see a renaissance in murder and slow murder. Many more monkey wrenches could be thrown into the electronic machinery; today's cyber attacks could be mild by comparison to tomorrow's.

International terrorism might grow two-fold or ten-fold. Even if we succeed in stamping out foreign-born threats, we could breed more than enough homegrown bombers and anthrax mailers to do us in. Increasing hordes of ordinary people could figure they've got to look out for themselves. Take any kind of job doing anything. Go into any kind of business pushing anything. Just so it pays the bills and takes care of the family. If it involves giving assistance to slow suicide, well, you don't really notice because your focus is closer to home; and "everyone's doing it." A perverted form of Adam Smith economics -- everyone looking out for their own self-interest -- could run rampant.

A mere worsening of intentional death is not the worst that can happen, however. Planetary extinction or near extinction is not unthinkable. We'd be wise to view the Earth as having a single mind. If the self-worth of that mind falls too low, where does that lead? If Earth's life stops seeming worthwhile to Earth, what's the obvious solution?

Choosing Life
Through Structural Change

The only way out may be the bold, thoroughly positive path of consciously maximizing our human qualities and leveraging the information age for human benefit. Let electronics take over our routine, structured mental functions; but don't let them take over us. Don't let a techno-elite displace us, mistakenly believing that the old fact still holds true, "There isn't enough for everyone."

Let's not let megatech "progress" ruin community and family life. And let's not let myopic fumbling ruin everything.

We need to affirm the new truth that -- thanks to centuries of discovery, creativity, and technical advance -- we now have the ability to make the world work for everyone. Let's develop and aggressively employ our unique aliveness and humanity. Go the conscious route; move up to a higher level. Not just some of us; all of us. Leave nobody out; that's lethal.

We need to do it individually and do it together. Personal change can accomplish a lot; survival requires social change as well. Mutual higher consciousness is the way out and up. But higher consciousness will spring to practical life only through the multiplying effect of metamind's reflective characteristic; that is, through the self looking at the self and intentionally making it become more of what it can be.

Unless we boost our consciousness to full-time, high-level metamind, we could be done for. We need to bear in mind, though, that higher consciousness (particularly its responsibility/love dimension) is a tricky thing. If limited in "width" or degraded in form, it can kill. And it will be limited unless our emotional safety valves are working. There are many, many things to fix.

The world has never been widely meta-conscious before. It's a huge challenge and we've got to get it right on the first try. But we can do it.

Society's prevailing consciousness has always been a narrow umbrella -- ideal for the tribe, OK for the farming community, tolerable for the industrial city, but no good for now. We need an umbrella as wide as the planet. We need to create unbounded global meta-consciousness, something foreign to us. Not so easy but worth a shot; and it's our only option.

Social changes described in this book will help it happen. Meanwhile, there is plenty we can do about it individually. Here are some suggestions:

- **Think of yourself as more than you.** Gradually strengthen the feeling that "you" are in fact your family, your work group or set of friends, your community, your professional association, your country, your world. If you were to die, you would not really be dead, because "you" continue to exist. This is in fact the perception of soldiers and fire fighters during heroic acts, and of advanced minds during moments of enlightenment.

- **Increase your tolerance.** If a Democrat, cut Republicans more slack; if a Republican, ditto for Democrats. Learn more about and gain a better understanding of people who may seem foreign: Jews, Christians or Muslims; gays, the sexually repressed, or the promiscuous; the poorly educated or homeless; members of the National Rifle Association or American Civil Liberties Union; perverts or criminals; terrorists. Protect yourself, of course, from those who might do harm; but don't condemn them. Remember, everyone is part of the larger "you," and you're not perfect. Think hard before labeling anyone fundamentally and irredeemably stupid, despicable, or evil.

- **Help others make transitions.** When a friend or associate loses a job or family member, the loss is also yours, because they're a part of the larger you. Adjusting isn't their responsibility alone; it's yours too, if you're fully human. Don't rest until they've got a new job or their life back on keel.

- **Engage in a mental or spiritual exercise,** such as prayer or meditation. Today's pressures have a way of beating on us until our consciousness narrows and love or shared consciousness all but disappears. We need a daily practice for rekindling the flame of aliveness.

- **Manage your consciousness better.** Notice more often and more deeply how you're feeling, what you're thinking, and where you're heading. Move your consciousness "up" a notch when it's down.

Life is our prized possession; and broad inclusive consciousness is life's source and substance. Intentional death will give way to it.

7

Restructuring a
Self-Destructing World

Making Society Meta-conscious

As we have seen in the past two chapters, survival and the future we want depend on being our best selves; and that involves strengthening the special qualities that make us human, particularly broad meta-consciousness.

It's hard to do that as individuals, all alone, however. We need to bolster our social infrastructure. This chapter suggests some fruitful avenues.

Better Tools of Interaction

Two things are critical for human intercourse: language and money. The first allows us to exchange ideas and instructions; the second, possessions and services. We need to improve both along metamental lines.

The problem with language is that we've got an excess of it: multiple languages that make communication and cooperation difficult across cultural lines. We need a single tongue that everyone understands.

Fortunately, we have a winning candidate: English. It's become the global standard for air traffic controllers and others whose jobs depend on instant, clear understanding. It's also the primary or second tongue for those who want to buy or sell globally: business managers, marketers, traders, transporters.

English is the clear winner because it's highly flexible and its words are highly ambiguous. As we saw in chapter 5, ambiguity (or the capacity to convey a variety of meanings in different contexts) is the attribute of language that makes it powerful. Through the years, English has refined a subset of 850 specific highly ambiguous words that can express any thought anyone can think.

Foreign-language speakers can start using English almost overnight simply by mastering Basic English, that set of 850 words. With the help of Basic English, English as a Second Language (ESL) instruction has become one of the hottest trends on the planet.

We're well on our way to a single global tongue thanks to Basic English. We can speed the process and all start singing on the same song sheet sooner if we --

- **Get everyone in American to use English as soon as possible**. We only extend separation when we offer core subjects such as math in Spanish or French.
- **Promote instruction in English as a Second Language.** It's already very popular in the U.S. and abroad.
- **Get better at Basic English ourselves.** Native speakers of English have vocabularies of 50,000 or more words. Most of the communications load, however, is carried by Basic English, that specific set of 850 words. The more flexibly and extensively you employ these words, the more powerfully you will think and communicate. A list of these words may be found on the Internet by entering, "basic English word list."
- **Learn at least a little of languages other than English.** It's common courtesy. You'll also communicate better across cultural divides and become a more successful world citizen.

As the information age matures and the brain drain progresses, we also need to bridge another language divide: that between people and ever-smarter electronic systems. Right now most of us don't understand electronic computation very well, and computer code "understands" us hardly at all.

A fruitful project would be to build Basic English into computing systems in a way that permits conversational understanding between us and our silicon siblings -- an extremely difficult task but one that would transform science, innovation, commerce and culture.

Money also needs to change along with our attitudes toward it and use of it. The money that greased the wheels of the industrial age has already changed into more fluid forms such as credit cards, direct deposits and money transfers, and online payment and collection systems such as PayPal. What other monetary innovations might we come up with?

Creative thinking could solve some of the problems we have with money today:

- **Too many people have too little money,** less than they need to live or be productive. An increasing number in America live below the poverty line.
- **Some people have much more money than they need,** not just millions but billions. It complicates their lives, separates them from others, and induces them to divert creativity and resources from serious problem solving to satisfy trivial luxury desires.
- **Most people have lost control over their money.** Tracking it has become increasingly complex and challenging.

Money is a symbolic medium like language. It is intended to smooth the transfer of goods, property, and services between people. What can we do differently to make those transfers smoother, more equitable, and synergistic?

Some of the recent money innovations have been a step backward, merely increasing the wealth gap. For example, easy credit and bait-and-switch interest rates on credit cards. One company charges 4.99% on unpaid balances but jumps the rate to 24.99% if a consumer makes a payment even one day late.

Better Government and Politics

Problems of citizenship and governance center, of course, on people. On one hand, not enough people participate. Voting rates are low, and volunteer public service has all but dried up. On the other hand, some people participate in overbearing ways, rigging this system in their favor.

How might the brain-drain and meta-consciousness trends be leveraged to improve the system? Might some public functions, such as recording votes, be taken over by the Internet? Might some of the procedures of public institutions be made more meta-conscious? For example, an alternative to the filibuster.

In addition, we need to develop specific govern-mental options for aiding human-edge job transition. Only through government can we establish the level playing field that the private sector needs to create new jobs and morph existing jobs into the new, better ones. We might consider --

- **Legislation and trade negotiations to moderate the pace of offshoring.** Which U.S. jobs are best sent overseas to India or China? Which are best kept here? And how can the rate of transfer be moderated to minimize transitional pain while higher-level, hyper-human jobs are created in the U.S.?

- **Review of tax policies.** Offshore workers pay no U.S. taxes, and the infrastructure supporting U.S. companies needs to be paid for by somebody. Congress might consider options such as tax breaks for laid-off white-collar workers who want to set up shop independently; or a U.S. analog of European tax policies that prevent an excessive wealth gap while generating much-needed revenues for social services and infrastructure.

- **Telecom reform** that brings last-mile bandwidth (vital for hyper-human information-age work) up to par with that of other key nations.

- **Federal job programs** that bring incomes to the displaced while strengthening the economy through rebuilding our physical and social infrastructure. There are myriad possibilities ranging from pollution cleanup to homeland security. To

175

improve our international stature as well as our security, one possibility might be a Social Army or greatly expanded Peace Corps to help foreign nations overcome health problems and poverty, incidentally defusing motivation for terrorism.

- **Implemention of an international minimum wage with global standards for health, safety and environmental protection.** As a result of the offshoring of service and technical work along with manufacturing, we're moving toward globalization of pay scales. Incomes will fall excessively low in the U.S. for many jobs, or the jobs simply won't be here without international props and a level playing field for employers.

The most significant change in politics could come through a shift from the mass to the personal. Today's top-down politics seeks to sway the many through promises, images, advertising, and PR. Personal politics would return us to earlier days of grass-roots involvement. A shift in that direction may already have started. In the 2004 Presidential campaign, use of the Internet, small-group meetings, and one-on-one networking has engaged the participation of many formerly alienated young people.

Personal versus mass politics would also blur the line between campaigning and governing. In a campaign high on the hyper-human scale, candidates would talk less about what they're going to do, and more about what they're already doing -- to empower their constituents and make a difference. Candidates would sweep into office on waves of volunteerism more than on waves of campaign expenditures.

Better Social & Economic Measures

To help us transition through the brain drain and technogreed trends to a meta-conscious society, we need better measurement tools. In moving up from today's know-how work to hyper-human work, we may need to start tracking the workforce using different measures. We may need to divide today's "service-sector" into two strands: know-how service work, being taken over by technology, and hyper-human service work done by people.

We may also find it advantageous to emphasize and track hyper-human forms of manual work that are performed with creativity and satisfaction. Examples include urban agriculture, specialized engineering, local production, artistic creation, and many varieties of nurturing.

The government or one of our think tanks might supplement current federal information gathering by tracking changes in hyper-human service employment, singled out from total service-sector employment.

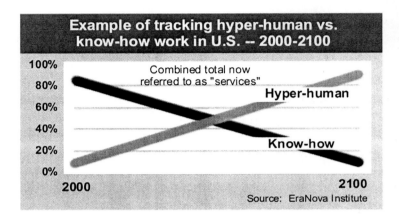

This would help us know how the *quality* of our service-sector jobs is changing, and how much know-how work is disappearing into automation.

There are several other things that might be tracked to help us better assess where we're going. These include --

- **The human value of our efforts,** through a Gross National Quality (GNQ) number as a supplementary and better measure of social well-being, environmental health, and economic progress than GNP, which tracks only the quantitative value of goods and services produced. (A basis for this might be the Index of Social Health published periodically by the Institute for Innovation in Social Policy at the Fordham University Graduate Center.)

- **Our informal economy,** in which we share things and services with family, friends, and colleagues without resorting to cash. (This "free" economy, harking back to ancient times, could expand greatly as hyper-human activity gains sway.)

- **Our progress toward national and international security,** which involves keeping tabs on two key factors: the people with motivation to do harm (through ideology or economic disadvantage), and the means to inflict catastrophic harm. Both are moving off the charts, and both need to be tracked to aid countermeasures.

Better Business

Some believe the U.S. is transitioning from an industrial society to something higher in the occupational pecking order: an "idea economy." Federal Reserve Board chairman Alan Greenspan has spoken of an America where value is no longer derived by creating and moving things, but by creating and moving ideas.

Surely this is a sound direction if "ideation" is appropriately defined. Ideation needs to be cultivated as more than ivory-tower thinking or board-room string-pulling. Ideas spring up close to where things happen -- in agriculture, manufacturing, and get-your-hands-dirty service work as well as in basic research, big-iron engineering, biotech development, or global marketing.

Former Secretary of State Henry Kissinger has warned that outsourcing could suck the innovative life out of America's industrial base. Ideas for improvement come from the factory workers, engineers, and managers where the work is done.

As more and more white-collar work, especially high-tech forms, is offshored, guess where the new ideas and intellectual property are likely to come from. Intel founder Andrew Grove has cautioned that tomorrow's most advanced engineering could come from India or China.

Idea generation needs to remain strong in America. In fact, it should grow stronger along with an accentuation of other hyper-human skills. Hyper-human skills flourish in active pursuits -- including food production, making things, and helping others -- where we engage our bodies, physical elements of the environment, feelings, and human interactions, not just airy thinking.

Better Non-profit Institutions

Government is essential for providing a framework or level playing field to let the next generation of better employment and life emerge. Government, however, is not the only facilitating influence.

Three additional powerful influences (philanthropy, volunteerism, and professional associations) are also relevant. Innovations to consider include --

- **A Super-rich Superfund.** The recent tax cut, going mainly to the rich, is supposed to create jobs. It could. If the top 10% invested their windfall and a fraction of their wealth to create hundreds of thousands of new businesses -- including micro-companies like those popular abroad -- the total infusion could dwarf the billions for rebuilding Iraq. This could release massive new wealth including millions of jobs, even if the majority of the new companies failed. The effect on the stock market could be enormous, restoring trillions in equity lost during the recent recession.

- **A redefinition of work to include volunteerism.** In the future we might decide that employment should be any activity that delivers value to others, not just paid work. We would then track, and thus encourage, more non-paid contribution by retired people, youngsters, and the well-to-do who need not work. Another possibility is to introduce compensation for volunteer work, for those who need it. This could consist of tax credits, health benefits, product coupons, service vouchers, or cash.

- **New empowerment for philanthropy.** Anyone who has ever given away sizeable amounts of money knows that it involves more than generosity. It also requires time, effort, skill, knowledge, and judgment -- not to mention responsibility. We might consider new ways to acknowledge and help supercharge charitable giving. In particular, ways to encourage the hyper-human aspects of giving -- creativity, involvement, vision, teaching, caring -- could be explored.

- **Refocused unions and professional associations** that work creatively with employers to create more good jobs with decent pay.

- **Bolstered consumer groups** that reward companies that provide good jobs as well as good products and services; and shun those that shed employees with abandon or introduce neo-sweatshop practices or poverty wages.

Better Education, Art Science and Culture

Our educational system can benefit from the more rapid introduction of programs for honing meta-consciousness. Already, cross-disciplinary programs in "thinking skills" are gaining popularity. Much more of this training is needed. To a large degree, education suffers from the continuation of industrial-age practices: production-line teaching, segmented categories of knowledge, and a focus on lower-level know-how that is being taken over by electronic systems.

At all levels, from kindergarten to graduate school, more solid training is needed in hyper-human areas:

- Basic thinking skills such as cross-disciplinary classification and operation analysis.
- Basic symbol systems including mathematics and English as thinking disciplines.
- Observation, problem spotting, and priority setting.
- Discovery including the scientific method.
- Creativity and innovation.
- Decision making.
- Planning, potential problem analysis, and control.
- Mood modification including emotional awareness and control.
- Motivation of others.
- Social organization and leadership.
- Communication in spoken, written, and cyber forms.
- Perceptual and motor skills involving the whole body and mind.
- Meta-consciousness and responsibility.
- Mastery over electronic and media influences (utilizing them without being dominated by them).
- Artistic and cultural creation and participation.
- Wealth production and management; creation of new value versus forms of money accumulation that divide people or harm the environment.

We also need to re-evaluate the trend toward standard-ized testing and instruction. It comes out of industrial-era thinking and is at odds with the hyper-human growth so vitally needed.

In addition, we have the chance to re-think our entire culture during the mind-into-electronics transfer. What are the opportunities for re-defining art, scientific discovery, and worship so as to promote new meta-conscious harmony and progress in society at large?

Tomorrow's Hyper-human Communities and Cities

The brain drain and meta-consciousness trends call for reinventing our cities, suburbia and agriculture.

What might be the form of our communities if designed meta-consciously and for the support of highly conscious people? So-called "intentional communities" already number in the hundreds. Mostly they're designed with social and ecological ends in mind. A new form, the "cyber-arcology" or "inter-community" is needed. It is an intentional community with broadband networking and other cyber features added, plus local agriculture (urban farming). It supports meta-conscious human activities while supply-ing the infrastructure for lower-level mental functions performed by electronic systems.

Existing cities such as New York, Chicago, London, and Tokyo have the potential of morphing into intercommunities and there are tentative signs of movement in that direction. Among the thousands of dying towns and depressed cities and suburban communities in America, many may have intercommunity potential.

A mature intercommunity will incorporate food production as well as electronic intelligence into its structure. Reliance on remote agriculture will be minimized. Internal transportation will be mostly human-powered, with mechanical transit reserved for movement between intercommunities. An intercommunity will combine residential functions with those of a university, cultural center, playground, school system, business park, and shopping center. The cyber component will facilitate rich, dynamic interactions between people within a single intercommunity, and between intercommunities.

In tomorrow's intercommunities, advertising will have morphed into a less invasive form and residents will enjoy old-fashioned face-to-face interaction in the spaces where they live, earn their livelihoods, and pursue cultural enrichment.

The Chautauqua Institution in New York has many elements of tomorrow's intercommunity, as does Arcosanti in New Mexico, and Celebration City in Florida. For more on the intercommunity concept and developments, see www.eranova.com/intercommunity.

Intercommunities will be part of a general process of rebuilding the local in harmony with the global. Healthy employment and community life require a fine-

tuning of globalization with a new emphasis on cohesive families, neighborhoods, towns and cities.

Re-thinking Small & Big

We need to reevaluate "local versus global" as well as
everything big versus everything small. Some things
are too excessive; others, too recessive.

Things that are too dominant (and often infected with
technogreed) include --

- **Multinational corporations** (disempowering
  small companies, employees, and communities).
- **Agribusiness** (displacing family farmers, producing ghost towns in middle America, and
  generating noxious pollution in the mass production of meat).
- **The military-industrial-congressional complex** (hurting defense as well as the economy
  through poorly audited, poorly controlled in-
  gestion of money, giving us systems that cost
  too much and work too poorly).
- **The federal government** (too controlled by
  mega-business and wealthy individuals through
  campaign contributions).
- **The auto** (burning excessive oil and money,
  and isolating people in bedroom communities).
- **Superstars** (making all but a handful of us into
  passive fans, watchers, and followers).

- **Advertising** (fast moving toward full-time mental influence).
- **Security, both national and in the home** (excessively draining resources from "real things" to pay for protection of the real things).
- **Mass production** (fostering big-iron solutions when small, local technology will do).

Things that are generally too small, not dominant enough, and in need of beefing up include --

- **Local communities** (too divided and impersonal, generally not dense enough for navigation by foot, and -- especially in rural areas -- too small and unvaried to be culturally alive in all ways).
- **Small, new businesses** (harder to start and more risky to run than necessary).
- **Grass-roots participation in local, state, and national government** (a majority of citizens have all but dropped out).
- **Local agriculture** (not enough nearby production of fresh vegetables, fruits, dairy products, chicken, and fish).
- **Walking and other forms of action in the normal activities of life** (a natural antidote to obesity and an alternative to time-consuming health clubs).
- **Trust and mutual support** (not enough of the sharing and open doors found in many small towns).

- **Self-reliance and pro-active buying** (too little self-empowerment in the face of monolithic advertising and consumerism).
- **Arts creation and performance by everyone** (not enough singing versus listening to super-stars sing, for example).
- **Local production of manufactured items to be used locally** (not enough neighborhood crafts or hand-made tools and appliances).

Globalization in its present form is the biggest "too big." Mindlessly pursued and tinged with technogreed, it can create enormous money concentration for a few while destroying overall wealth, killing communities, distorting economies, taxing the environment, and of course disrupting employment and lives.

Global trade makes sense for many items, of course. But global everything will kill the globe. Local is where people live and it should be the center of all vital activities, including the growing of food and the making of things. We need to ask, "Which goods are best produced a mile away rather than a continent away? Which foods are best grown within walking distance rather than trucking or flying distance?"

Global Metamind?

While local is our core, it finds its complete expression in a healthy connection to the global.

A far-out social development, predicted half a century ago by philosopher Teilhard de Chardin, could emerge many years hence if we survive the electronic brain drain and succeed in creating a world that works.

Teilhard called it the "noosphere," a planetary consciousness encompassing the aggregate awareness of millions of peaceful, collaborating humans. According to Teilhard, a Jesuit Priest as well as geologist and paleontologist, the phenomenon will come about with a technological assist.

Next Steps

Through a multi-disciplinary effort involving major universities, corporations, governmental agencies, and foundations, the brain drain and technogreed problems need to be thoroughly investigated and defined; and solutions need to be developed and implemented by business, governmental, and non-profit organizations as well as individuals.

A "human edge institute" might be created to assume this task. (A paper on this is available at www.eranova.com.)

There is a lot we need to do to clear the chasm of oblivion to land on the next higher level for society. Above all, in light of the mounting transfer of know-how tasks into electronic systems, we need to recognize that the winning strategy for the information age is to inject "aliveness" -- including deliberate reflection -- into everything we do; let electronic systems take over the dead, dull stuff; and leave technogreed behind.

8

Transforming the Commercial Chameleon

Restoring the Human Color of Business

In many ways, America's large companies are quite wonderful: efficient, flexible, and profitable. They deliver value to their customers and income to millions of employees and stockholders. But there's a problem with them, a problem that's solvable but quite serious. The aim of this chapter is to lay out a solution path.

The problem appears to strengthen large corporations short term but undermines their futures while making life difficult for smaller companies. The problem creates piles of private money but flushes general wealth down the drain. The problem also threatens millions of employees, our public institutions, our lifestyles and values, and our lives.

The problem is technogreed. As manifested in many if not most large corporations today, technogreed is more than simple greed latched onto technology. It's a complex, seemingly inevitable way of operating: a roaring train that says with its very momentum, "I'm what's happening; get out of my way." In today's mega-business, technogreed reveals itself in three deadly errors:

- Confusion over who the company is.
- Confusion over who the customer is.
- Domination over other social forms.

Who Is the Company?

Note that I say *who*, not *what*. Companies started out not as abstract entities but as groups of people joined together for a common purpose. For example: Shakespeare's company of players.

Early companies were more like families than like today's GM, Verizon, or CitiGroup. Though the company existed to serve customers, it existed more fundamentally to serve its members, for the company *was* its members. As a leader of an early company, you would hesitate to take advantage of or jettison an associate. That would be like oppressing or banishing one of your own children. (Today in countries like Albania thousands of poor families rent or sell their children, but we of course deplore the practice.)

Somewhere along the line, our larger companies stopped being family-like assemblages of people. A sales executive I know laments the death of the personnel department in favor of the human resources department. Employees, the former company members, have become "resources" -- expendable commodities like raw materials, parts, supplies, or energy. To the extent that the "company" still consists of a human assemblage, it has shrunk to senior management and a few others. Everybody else can be dispensed with in hard times.

This is in stark contrast to the "company" in the army. This "company" is a specific, unified group of soldiers. It consists of real live bodies and souls -- not a conceptual entitity that can casually change its form. In an army company you don't abandon some of the troops when the going gets tough or rations run low. Everybody hangs together. (Without this bonding, would you expect soldiers to have the strong will to fight referred to in chapter 6?)

In addition to becoming less defined as a specific assemblage of people, today's large company has also became more and more of a legal fiction: a logo propped up by ad campaigns behind which even the CEO could disappear without notice.

A good example is AT&T. Who is AT&T? That's a very hard question to answer because the cast of characters keeps changing. As a consultant to AT&T for almost 10 years, I witnessed:

- The jettisoning of thousands of employees in wave after wave.
- The departure of four CEOs.

- The selling off of the NCR computer operation.
- The acquisition and then the splitting off of the cable operation that was supposed to be AT&T's new future.
- The spinning off of most of AT&T Labs.
- The creation and then the divestiture of a wireless business (AT&T Wireless).

What is AT&T "really"? Not exactly a specific group of people. Most of the managers, engineers, and scientists I worked with are no longer there. The work-force is a shadow of its former self; and the leadership is all new faces. What remains of AT&T is basically its logo -- its image or story.

Our mega-companies aren't "people" anymore. They're real-seeming phantoms that process money. People inhabit them in fleeting clumps that quickly disband and vanish.

This might be okay if all the people in the transient clumps got their fair share of the processed money. But they're not getting it. More and more of the money is going to those who already have most to start with. And the brain-drain trend promises to accentuate this transfer since our electronically-powered legal fictions are requiring fewer and fewer human resources.

Who Is the Customer?

This is the second deadly confusion in big business today. In a literal, superficial sense, customers are still well attended to, and corporate America knows exactly who the customers are and how to motivate them. They're the ones who plunk down their money for the SUV's, the beer, the toothpaste, the insurance.

The confusion is revealed when you follow the money. In a healthy business environment, money comes to vendors through free-will decisions made by customers. Visualize an open-air marketplace: lots of people at stands selling fruit, vegetables, fish, garments, arts and crafts; lots of people milling around looking at all the stuff for sale, comparing prices and quality; money and goods changing hands. Period.

It's not so simple in big business today. If a "customer" is defined as the one who gives you money, then there are two new "customers" that divert attention from the real customer.

The stock market as customer: Through stock options and other perks, the people who really matter in big companies, CEOs, can make more money through pleasing Wall Street than through pleasing customers.

Of course they must please customers in order to please Wall Street, or so the argument goes. But in practice Wall Street seems to care more about short-term gains than long-term corporate health. So executives cut corners or people. With varying degrees of their own and investors' technogreed, they --

- Cook the books, as at Enron.
- Or merely miss opportunities, as at AT&T.

Some executives somehow succeed in balancing con-
flicting demands for good results all around, though I
cannot produce a totally clean example.

The government as customer: Money goes to Washington because money comes from Washington.
Support candidates and they will support you by
conferring commercial advantage. Laws, regulations,
licenses, tariffs, and other governmental instruments act
as modifiers of the pristine marketplace. They sometimes set a level playing field, serving the interests of
buyers and sellers alike. At other times they --

- Confer or preserve monopoly or monopoly-like
  power over buyers (as in today's drug pricing
  and availability).
- Favor bigger businesses over smaller ones (as in
  the bankrupting of family farmers in favor of
  agribusiness).
- Cost taxpayers billions by permitting pollution
  (as in the production of chemicals, steel, meat,
  and countless other products).

Note that the misapplied attention to these two non-
customer "customers" happens predominantly in our
larger companies. Though as susceptible to greed as
anyone, entrepreneurs and small-company managers
generally have the luxury of giving undivided attention
to real customers. Having not yet gone public or gained
big-guy clout, they escape the diversions of Wall Street
and Washington alike.

There is another error in big-company customer con-sciousness. That is the fact that the employee is also a customer. Henry Ford realized this, insisting on paying his factory workers enough so they could afford to buy the cars they built. Wal-Mart, for one, seems to have lost sight of this, paying its average worker less than a poverty-level wage (for a family of three).

Today's big company has become like a schizo-phrenic holdup man and street vendor in one skin. "Give me your wallet ... now buy my trinkets."

Big Companies Have Become Too Dominant

Big business is often equated with free enterprise, which in turn is equated with a free society. But small business, now challenged by big business, is a freer form of free enterprise. And free enterprise (business) is only one part of a free society. The others are:

- **The family**
- **The community**
- **County, state and federal governments**
- **Non-profit "companies"** (human aggegations including religious groups, educational institutions, volunteer fire departments, professional associations, philanthropies, and helping organizations of all types)

Big business has gotten much too dominant and over-powering, disempowering the other components of our free society, including small business. Money as distinct from value seems to have bceome the life blood of America, and the primary money funnel is big business. Here are some of its negative impacts:

The family has gotten smaller and weaker. The average household size is down to three. Having bought in to the industrial-era idea of working for someone else, we've lost the knack of growing our own food or making our own things. Busy with increased workloads or the frantic need to find new employment, we spend less time eating together or talking to one another or doing things as a family team. There are fewer occasions for the emotional expression that keeps people healthy, human, and productive.

Many communities are disintegrating. Factory jobs go overseas and whole towns dry up. A big chain store moves in and the downtown market or drug store goes under.

Government by the people is weaker -- though government is strong. Ordinary citizens, especially racial minorities and the financially pressed, have been opting out of the voting booth. Only 55% of the voting-age population voted in the 2000 Presidential election; rates have been much lower, 40% and below, in non-presidential election years. Maybe a lot of people are too busy to pay attention to politics, or find it hard to get to the polls because they're working two jobs. Or maybe they figure government has been bought by business anyway.

Non-profit organizations are suffering. The philanthropic engine is humming, delivering billions to worthy causes. However, many needs are going unmet and volunteerism is down. People seem too stressed to give a hand as they once did. The business sector demands more and more frantic activity in spite of the spectre of massive job dislocation.

What's the Solution?

Business has morphed into something it wasn't at the time of Ben Franklin. It's a chameleon that's changed it's colors radically and its grown from a little guy to a Godzilla. We can't change it back to the way it was but we can make it more profitable for everyone, not just a minority.

How? We need to provoke a national dialog and input from experts in many fields. For starters, I'll offer a general strategy and a few suggestions. The general strategy is simple:

- **Understand and agree on the problem.** Big business has gotten too dominant and infected with an excess of technogreed.
- **Tame the excesses of big business and make it more fit for people.** Emphasize hyper-human skills rather than treating people as commodities

to be replaced as soon as possible by electronics.

Here are my specific suggestions, just a few among many that might come from many quarters.

► **Suggestion 1: Go easy on offshoring.** Management consulting firms are currently telling executives they have no choice but to offshore thousands of U.S. jobs to low-paid foreign professionals. This advice, seemingly practical and necessary in the short term, carries dangers to longer-term stability and growth: white-collar union organizing; employee backlash such as activism and cyber attacks; and a sputtering consumer engine that could threaten the continued existence of many large, venerable companies.

► **Suggestion 2: To improve a single company, improve all companies.** It's hard for individual firms to justify expensive reforms that put them at a competitive disadvantage. They need to lobby Washington for a better level playing field, reducing the immediate pressing need to cut costs -- mostly people costs -- through white-collar offshoring, export of manual work, or restructuring. Business doesn't have to be the way business is. It can be designed, like anything else, to be the way we'd like it to be. And it's got to be better for people than it is now, or the game ends.

► **Suggestion 3: Re-define existing jobs.** Some forward-looking companies are adding hyper-human tasks to existing jobs, making them more productive and less susceptible to automation or offshoring. (There's an example in chapter 10.) Adding hyper-human tasks involves job redefinition, new policies, and training to spark innovation, intrapreneurship, teamwork, and focus on customer needs. Some resources are available for accomplishing this; others need to be developed.

► **Suggestion 4**: **Automate in tandem with hyper-human job creation.** Automation that replaces people leads to trauma of change, often months and sometimes years of little or no income. However, automation complemented by a parallel creation of new, better jobs hurts no one and confers benefits all around. Leading companies will strive for this win-win approach to productivity improvement, remembering that there's no longer any new place for people to go, other than to hyper-human work.

► **Suggestion 5**: **Put increased emphasis on "mental models" and the seven metamind skills in chapter 7.** The hallmark of hyper-human work is practical reflection or self-guidance of one's thoughts and per-formance. It's vital to give employees training, job aids, and electronic tools for applying mental models to increase their effectiveness in product development, sales and marketing, management, and other areas. Doing so can create billions in new wealth. (See chapter 10.)

Overall, business leaders can lead the employment revolution by creating the next generation of jobs, based more on human-edge skills than on skills assumable by electronic technology.

Otherwise companies will be the victims of union resurgence, professional associations turned militant, legislative constraints, and activism of all sorts. Vandalism by angry employees is already a concern of corporate security departments. So is cyber-vandalism. And as some displaced professionals adopt Ted Kaczynski-like attitudes, home-grown terrorism could flourish. These dangers can be averted through steps such as those suggested here.

Many executives realize that running a large company is not just about making money or making stockholders happy, and not even just about making customers happy. It's about serving society, building community, and improving the general lot of everyone. That includes serving the needs of employees and building sound corporate cultures.

The future may belong to companies like GE, 3M, and IBM that -- recent aberrations aside -- have traditionally placed a high value on customer service, innovation, teamwork, community citizenship, and constant improvement with minimum human casualty.

It's time for corporate America to place a new emphasis on human-centered business practices, training and development, and electronic systems that empower rather than harass employees and customers alike. It might be called "corporate aliveness," and of course involves leveraging hyper-human skills in new wealth-producing ways.

Through corporate aliveness, more jobs will be recast to include the "aliveness" qualities exhibited by entrepreneurs, inventors, authors, composers, teachers, and others who like to be creative, do good, and empower others.

Sound corporate principles can be maintained even in conjunction with practices such as offshoring. For example, in early 2003, JP Morgan Chase announced that it would move part of its research work -- preparation of stock market reports -- to India. No U.S. workers would be laid off, they said, but freed up to focus on customers and high-level financial analysis. It's the winning strategy if they live up to it.

The most significant positive change in corporate America would be the emergence of high responsibility and courage at the top. America's Medal of Honor recipients have been described as people who love life so much they are prepared to die for it. They transcend themselves and win our admiration.

It has been said that today's CEOs deserve their multi-million-dollar annual compensation even when laying off thousands, and that "you have to offer big bucks or you won't get the best people." Maybe, but perhaps the best people can't be bought.

We need more business leaders like Lee Iaccoca and John Reed:

- In 2003 the New York Stock Exchange was criticized for poor oversight and largesse at the top. Chairman Dick Grasso's pay was $149 million. John Reed, former head of Citicorp, agreed to straighten things out as interim chairman for $1.

- In 1979 when the world economy was in trouble and Chrysler was in danger of going under, President Lee Iacocca cut his salary to $1 a year. He also asked everyone in management to take a pay cut -- except for the secretaries, who deserved every cent of their pay in his view.

9

Mediamorphosis

*Changing Communications to
Support a Meta-conscious Society*

In 1990 the World Wide Web did not exist. The first
WWW code was released by Tim Berners-Lee in 1991.
Now, as I write this in 2003, the Web is everywhere,
fast becoming the central organizing force of industry,
communications, commerce, entertainment and more.

In a similar brief span something new and just as
revolutionary is going to take over the world. What?
My candidate is universal interaction or UI.

Universal interaction is a coming transformation in
the way we communicate, watch TV and listen to
music, buy and sell, teach and learn, create and decide,
travel, work, and live. Depending on how we roll it out
and adapt to it, UI can give us great new power and
freedom, or make us irrelevant and impotent. Rolled

out right, UI will strongly support and enable our growing meta-consciousness.

Riding the next-new-thing bandwagon, several infocom heavyweights are pushing UI infrastructure, but few people -- even among the heavyweights -- fully appreciate UI's Promethean promise and pitfalls.

Universal interaction, not quite here but soon to surround us, is just what the name suggests: the universal, persistent ability to be personally connected for any media exchange, transaction, physical activity, or other interaction that involves any network anywhere on the planet. Instant, effortless communication; being virtually anywhere and doing virtually anything. Eyes, ears, and arms that span the planet. That's UI.

Think of it as the Web Part 2, except it's much more than something you do sitting at a PC. UI components including embedded chips, wireless transmissions, and code will be everywhere and will mediate everything: phone calls, purchases in stores, trips by auto and air, instruction of many types, the operation of home appliances, corporate accounting, home heating and lighting, manufacturing and inventory control, space exploration, homeland security.

Nobody is saying, "Let's push UI," but it's arriving bit by bit, and big outfits are promoting the infrastructure to support it. UI's enabling technologies are the hottest new things around. They include --

- **Web Services software** from Microsoft, IBM, Sun and others. This lets companies easily automate intra-company interactions of all types, from selling and sourcing to manufacturing and servicing.

- **On-demand computing,** a service now offered by IBM, Hewlett-Packard, Microsoft and Sun. It lets companies and potentially individuals share computer resources via the Internet -- in effect turning computer usage into a ubiquitous utility like electricity or water. From anywhere on the planet, turn on a trickle, or turn on a super-computer surge -- whatever you need. Last year IBM grossed $7 billion from its on-demand services.

- **Self-aware computing,** being developed by IBM and DARPA (the Defense Advanced Research Projects Agency). This smart code "knows what it's doing" and can correct itself, like a person, as it goes along.

- **Machine vision,** now used to control robotic systems for drug discovery, gene sequencing, and quality assurance. Offering human-like perception and physical manipulation, this technology will find its way into many industrial, commercial, and home applications. Few machine-vision devices will look like robots, but they'll perform robotic functions such as opening and closing things, assembling components, inspecting and sorting produce or merchandise, determining when something seems "right" or needs attention.

- **Radio frequency identification (RFID) tags,** which consist of silicon chips and a tiny antenna that can send data to a wireless receiver. They convey information as bar codes do, but through the air and on the fly at a distance. They're now used in autos for automatic toll collection; and Wal-Mart is forcing its suppliers to add the grain-of-sand-sized tags to their products. The aim is to streamline inventory tracking and supply-chain intelligence. Soon RFID's will be in our sneakers, cereal boxes, luggage, road signs, appliances, lawns, and magazines. Many of us will walk around with RFID identity tags that automatically open doors for us, log us on to networks, or speed us through security checkpoints. These pervasive identifiers will give a kind of sensory perception to smart computer networks spanning the planet.

All of these technologies cohabit the global Internet, and they give electronic technology awesome new autonomous powers. Yet more revolutionary change will come from --

- Biotechnology that is moving into computational and industrial applications.
- Photonic computing.

- Nanotechnology, or engineering at the atomic level.

Think of the planet as a body that's growing a nervous system with billions of tiny organs to sense what's happening and where everything is, and billions of hands to move things around. Some of the sensing and manipulating will be done automatically; some will be directed by humans. Now here's the big question:

Will UI be directed mostly by a privileged elite?
Or will all of us have free access to the controls?

Put another way, will most of us be pullers of the important strings; or puppets on strings pulled by others?

Isn't interactivity great?

Put yet another way, are we heading -- by design or default -- toward the extermination of the human race in favor of smart electronic descendants; or do we aim to be the living intelligence in charge of everything?

Universal interaction is almost here; bits and pieces of it already exist. Let's assemble the remaining pieces with extreme care. Are we going to build a universal interaction system that truly liberates and empowers us, or one that delivers universal domination or exclusion?

We need to decide. We need to intentionally create the system we want. Otherwise, by default technogreed will disenfranchise the majority in the near term, and wreck everything longer term.

How to Build UI Right

For starters, we need to find a way to assure a decent income for everyone, so people can attend to living rather than lashing out at a system that seems bent on displacing them. Creating this new pattern of universal income won't be easy since most of today's tasks are going to run on automatic, but it must be done.

Then we need to construct a global, democratic, all-empowering UI infrastructure. This is a matter of social engineering more than electronic engineering. For the system to be socially viable, its goal cannot be today's big-company goal: maximum profit filtered to the top at whatever seemingly necessary human cost. The ultimate payoff will be disaster.

Let's start by getting our priorities straight. What's the most valuable thing on earth? Not productivity. Not ownership or wealth. Not dumb robotic systems, however complex and elegant. Aliveness. That's what's most valuable. Human aliveness and its core quality: broad, inclusive self-awareness.

Our key aim must be to support metamind. We need to create a UI system that is optimized for broad, democratic mind extension, not mind replacement. We need to engineer individual control in at least three key areas: perception and motor control, personal identity or who we are, and how we think and are informed.

- 1 -

IN CONTROL OF OUR
GLOBAL EYES AND EARS

Right now the Internet, TV, radio, and print media offer many impressive mind-extending capabilities ranging from electronic dictionaries to camera eyes that extend our vision to Africa or the surface of Mars. Compared to what is possible, though, the global network does little to support our thinking, perception, or creative action. Electronic mind extension is in its infancy, currently very minimal. What might a more supportive global mind do for us?

For one thing, it could give us global muscles as well as global eyes and ears. In effect, our physical reach would span the globe and extend into space.

Arms 3,000 Miles Long

When we listen to the radio or watch TV, we do just that -- listen and watch. In physical life, by contrast, we go beyond passive observation. We look and listen, then respond with action. We hear and see and feel, then do something with our muscles. We move feet, hands, and lips to move the world around us. Motor functions complete the sensory-motor dynamic duo.

The global network will be more of a true mind extender when it lets us not only perceive at a distance but also make things happen at a distance. With the telephone, we've had this capability for decades. With a phone, you listen and then you talk, and the talking makes all the difference.

The Mighty Distance-spanning Phone

When you talk on the phone, you give advice, make requests, and give orders. Then things happen on the other end, miles away. It's magic! Sales are made, relationships formed, events and industries created. Today's national and global economies owe their existence partly to rapid transportation but more, I believe, to rapid, distance-bridging communication, notably talking by phone.

A next great leap for the Internet and all visual and tactile media is to add the motor dimension to the sensory. Speech is one means of directing remote action; control by hands or feet is another means; body language (pointing or frowning or smiling) is yet another; and so is showing by diagram, picture, or example. In the realm of make-believe, computer games already let us control events with joysticks and keyboards. We can easily imagine similar sensory-motor interactivity finding its way into adult entertainment including sitcoms, movies, and computer-generated music.

Real Clout in the Real World

Beyond make-believe media, the real world of action offers rich opportunities for remote control. With a steering wheel in your living room and live audio/visual feedback from a PC, there is no reason you couldn't drive a delivery truck remotely, from thousands of miles away.

Imagine electronic sensors and controls all over the place. You could be anywhere and do anything anywhere else: be in Miami and perform surgery in Chicago; be in Boston and evacuate a burning building in Bombay; be on a space station and tutor your kids in Spain.

The emerging e-home will be an early site for adding remote motor control. The kitchen lights are on and you want them off? You're in the bedroom? Turn off the kitchen lights from your bed. You're away on vacation? Turn off the kitchen lights from the beach or mountains.

- 2 -

IN CONTROL OF WHO WE ARE

There's a new kind of "reflection" that is just now starting to materialize. Remember that reflection is meta-consciousness or mind aware of mind. Now there's starting to be an electronic "metamind" or new instance of you, stored in the network.

Call that new you "e-me," an electronic representation of you. It will be complemented by similar representation of broader entities: "e-home," "e-community," "e-company," "e-product," "e-government," and so on.

The earliest element of "e-me" was the telephone number -- a network-based identifier that could be used to locate and connect to you. Other more recent elements of "e-me" are the e-mail address, personal web home page, network address book, network calendar, and so on. Telephone voice messages are also elements of e-me, as are email messages, and documents such as reports or photographs you may store in the network. E-me includes everything about you and for you stored in electronic form and accessible through the network. In time it may include your complete personal history, all your financial and medical information, your life's creative output, your complete personal genome, and more -- including, of course, your money, intellectual property, and network-accessible physical possessions.

When you die, your e-me will live on for as long as others find value in it. This e-me or reflection of you may be much more than a fond memory. If you leave behind network-stored knowledge and skills, these may be called upon just as others now call upon you yourself for input or services. If you're a skilled heart surgeon, for example, your e-me may be consulted by colleagues years after the "real you" is gone.

Once UI infrastructure is mature, the e-me function will be quite robust and constantly active in your interests (or to your detriment). While you're living, e-me will be your intermediary for all network-based interactions; and e-me will represent you to others, acting as agent, screener, privacy protector, and more. E-me will be active in your stead all the time. If positively implemented, it will look out for your interests while you're playing golf, eating dinner, and sleeping. And when you yourself interact with your e-me, it will have the capacity to extend your mind and action in powerful ways we are only beginning to imagine.

On the other hand, if negatively developed, your e-me will manipulate you many times more powerfully than today's advertising and PR. It will spy on you, make you the pawn of corporate or government designs, severely limit your freedom, or lead you in directions you don't want to go.

We could try to stop e-me technology from proliferating, but that won't work. Bits and pieces of it are already here, and it's going to be here full force unless technology stops developing altogether. Our only choice, other than reverting to a non-technological society, is to develop e-me right. You in charge of your e-me. Me in charge of mine.

E-me is the basic and most important element of the new electronic meta-reflection of the real world; but there's going to be an e-everything, and we've got to make sure it doesn't deprive us of our hard-won freedom and synergistic relationships.

E-home technology, now being developed by Microsoft and others, will be the "reflection" of a household. It will serve family members as a group as well as individually, extending sensory and other mental powers. For example, cameras and microphones in the home will serve as "eyes" and "ears" that let you monitor utilities and activities when you're traveling. When I was consulting with AT&T's developers of the "home of the future," a camera snapped a picture of the home's entryway every time the doorbell rang. These photos could be viewed remotely over the Internet to check on visitors or possible intruders.

E-community technology will provide electronic intelligence that lets people live together more harmoniously, efficiently, and creatively in neighborhoods, towns, and cities. It will make goods, utilities, services, and cultural events more accessible -- eventually cutting to near zero the need for auto traffic within the living areas of communities.

E-company, e-product, and e-government technology will similarly transform the functioning of public institutions and businesses. We need to build these things right. The present ad-hoc approach isn't good enough.

- 3 -

IN CONTROL OF OUR MINDS

Enormous resources are being invested to transfer mental functions into electronic systems. Too much of this merely replaces people. We need a greater proportion that extends thinking without undermining the thinker. Two examples:

- **Management decision support systems.** This profit-enhancing software supports rather than supplanting decision makers by acting as data gofer, displayer of alternatives, and calculator of weighted values. The manager does the real thinking and supplies the all-important responsibility and judgment.

- **A proposed massive database of "compressed experiences,"** based on successes and failures in business and government. This unibuitous system would be an "alternate reality" of real-world experiences and findings. It would be patterned after the Harvard case method and decision simulations I developed for IBM several years ago. Managers facing a problem would test out their thinking on a similar situation from the past. The payoff: simulated goofs rather than real ones, with millions of dollars saved or gained, perhaps lives saved as well.

I cannot stress too much the need to serve the mind rather than replace it. The opposite approach is much too strongly embedded in current thinking and practices. For example, a leading Internet researcher recently told me, "Developers of Web Services strive for zero, that is, zero people."

Flip Side of AI

Electronic mind extension is the neglected, little-noticed flip side of automation and artificial intelligence (AI), and its aim is *not* to increase profits by cutting human costs. It makes us smarter rather than making computers smart like us. (I use AI in a broad sense to include any technology that makes electronic systems behave like humans.) While AI and automation substitute for human thought, electronic mind extension empowers people and extends individual effectiveness.

A robust, universally accessible mind-support system would transform the way individuals, companies, governments, and societies interact, solve problems, survive, and progress. It has the power to greatly boost innovation and productivity, helping to spawn the global renaissance we all want.

Two separate developments, electronics and mind-training, have each to some degree already extended the practical output of the mind. Now the two, traveling on separate tracks, are ready to come together synergistically to make a profound difference in how we use our heads and get things done.

On the electronics track, the groundwork has been laid by the rise of global networks; pervasive computing; and developments such as speech recognition and databases that smooth interactions between people.

On the mind-training track, recent psychological, neurological, physiological, and educational advances have defined the structure and content for electronic mind extension. We now know a lot about what it takes for people to come up with new ideas, evaluate evidence and find causes, make sound decisions, develop plans relatively free of potential problems, manage emotions, and then embolden themselves for action and gain the cooperation of others.

Most current offerings relevant to electronic mind extension -- decision-support tools, creativity joggers, design tools, simulators, and search engines -- have flaws that make them less than ideal for everyday use. They're commonly too complex for ordinary people; too inconvenient or unreliable; too insulting (a dumb system telling a smart person what to do); or, as with search engines, they miss opportunities to link results to appropriate phases of human thought such as creativity or assessing consequences.

Many are nice in theory but toylike in practice. In addition, current offerings cover only a fraction of the mind-action waterfront.

Practical Steps

The basic opportunity is to aggregate research and promote the creation of a practical, user-tested, pervasive system that really helps people think better and do better, as compressed experiences have in paper-and-pencil form.

An additional opportunity is to facilitate the harnessing of "mental robots" or agents to perform simple functions autonomously according to the user's prescriptions, all for the user's benefit.

Phases of the construction of a global mind-extension support system include --

- Creating the software component.
- Creating the physical (network and device) component.
- Perfecting the mental component (developing training for the effective use of the software and physical components).

Applications using mind extension methods and authoring tools might include:

- Mind support for business and governmental managers (in small to large organizations).
- Business-to-business and business-to-consumer support.

- Specialized industrial and commercial applications.
- Interaction support including shopping and investment support.
- "Life" support and home automation support.
- Educational support.
- Smartened database, word processing, spreadsheet, and speech-recognition applications.
- All kinds of mind-mediated media and informational applications.

The value and impact of the electronic mind extension category cannot be overemphasized. Almost all past progress has been the result of human action directed by human thought; but until now, thinking has been ad-hoc, and the mind, grossly underutilized.

With electronic mind extension, magnified, enhanced, globally supported human intelligence could be the highest fulfillment of the computer and networking revolution.

It would be a powerful catalyst for provoking more frequent, higher-quality states of meta-consciousness. It's one of the infrastructure developments that together could revolutionize business, science, political and social interaction, the arts, education, everything.

10

Wealth-creating Opportunities

Mega-gold in Metamind

This chapter offers a perspective for entrepreneurs, managers, scientists, engineers, investors, and others who want to create wealth for themselves, associates, and society at large. The perspective involves leveraging the concept of metamind in key areas where money changes hands.

Creating wealth, true wealth, involves making money but differs from it. You can make money while destroying wealth. An example is cornering the market on seed corn and then selling it as food, never planting any of the seeds to create more corn. You may do well in the short run, but the supply of corn diminishes and everyone suffers in the long run. Another example is the one-time mass harvesting and near extermination of America's buffalo.

Much of today's wealth accumulation is of this sort. A few individuals like the captains of Enron get rich by cornering money or depleting a resource while creating nothing. They are in fact net destroyers of wealth. It's ironic, but wealth destruction often goes along with getting rich. It's a glitch in the use of our symbol system for exchanging things: money.

What Is Wealth, Really?

Seed planting is a good metaphor for the creation of true wealth. You multiply something useful in endless cycles of proliferation. Technology, except when employed with technogreed, works like seed planting except the seeds get better and better.

The improved seeds produce twice the quantity, then three times, then five, then nine, then twenty, and so on. Buckminster Fuller calls this technological process "more-with-lessing," the constant creation of more results with less and less material and energy. The best example is the microchip which continues to undergo geometric leaps in performance.

In defining wealth, Fuller invokes Einstein's famous formula, $E=mc2$. Energy and mass are equivalent and interchangeable, and the sum total can never be diminished. The substance of the universe can't be used up; by using it we merely transform it. It's still there to nourish us, clothe us, shelter us, protect us, and move us around. It never goes away and for all practical purposes, it's infinite.

This energy and mass, the "stuff" of our world, is one component of wealth. The other is intelligence, the mental stuff that lets us utilize the physical stuff in successive cycles of leverage and advantage. Intelligence, when used, increases. Matter and energy, when used, are conserved. Therefore, wealth can only grow as intelligence is applied to matter/energy; and the faster intelligence is applied, the faster wealth grows.

This is in fact what has happened in the past few centuries as technology has taken hold. Today millions of us eat better than yesterday's kings and queens; and we're on the threshold of producing that happy circumstance for everyone on the planet.

But there's a problem. Intelligence must be applied in pure, unadulterated form. If tinged with greed such as today's rampant technogreed, intelligence succeeds in diverting money but often falters in creating the "better seeds" that sprout into ever-greater true wealth.

If you want to create wealth, the first step is to be clear about what wealth is: more with less, not the mere cornering of money. The second step is to focus on an area of need and opportunity. The third is to apply the seven elements of metamind.

To create wealth today ...

1. Be clear about what wealth is: more with less, for all.
2. Focus on an area of need and opportunity.
3. Apply the seven elements of metamind.

Humans excel at ...	E-systems excel at ...
METAMIND **MICRO SKILLS** 1. Basic thinking skills and symbolism. **MACRO SKILLS** 2. Conscious monitoring and control (perceptual and motor). 3. Hypothesizing. 4. Creativity and imagination. 5. Subjective decision making. 6. Social skills. 7. Responsibility (valuing, love, and pursuit of ethical objectives).	**DEFINED OPERATIONS** • Number crunching and routine logic. • Mass storage and retrieval. • Remote sensing and control. • Structured or routine decision making. • Control of repetitive processes. • Simple or labor-intensive instruction.

225

TAKING STEP 1

Your product, service or project must deliver real value; and over time, more and more value. This is easier said than done, however, for all who produce goods and services are infected by some trace of technogreed, as are all their customers. For example, the production of sports cars selling for $600,000 eats up creativity and resources that might be applied to ending starvation in Botswana. The sports cars deliver "value" of a sort to millionaires, but *value* has many possible meanings.

Part of being clear about the nature of wealth is to be clear about who it's for. A narrow set of people? A larger set? Or everyone on the planet? Who you decide the wealth is for will determine what products or services you focus on. If you agree that our future depends on achieving "enough" for everyone, then you'll probably set your sights very wide.

Actually doing so may be extremely difficult, however. For example, in America's breadbasket, most farmers produce a narrow set of products: soybeans, corn, oats, and wheat. If you're driving through Kansas and expecting to find a farmer's market, you're likely to be disappointed. In the farm belt it's no longer profitable, ironically, to farm a wide variety of produce -- things like lettuce, string beans, cantaloupe, grapes, or squash. The Government subsidy program, of course, is what makes it so.

Moral: If you want to have full latitude in choosing the wealth-producing products or services to focus on, you may have to be politically active.

There's another fact about wealth and money that should be understood if you want to create more-with-less today. Money may be going away as wealth starts to grow geometrically. Once there's "enough" for everyone, who needs money? Just give what you have and take what you need.

Among our young people there is already the feeling that everything on the Internet -- information, software, music -- ought to be free. How about fruits and vegetables? Should they be free too? Well, they already are in spots. Many summer gardeners share their excess with friends; and in some Midwestern post offices you'll find free tomatoes, corn, and beans left there by residents with more than enough.

A 100% *free* free enterprise for most items is entirely practical in a world of plenty, but I won't take space to describe it here. For a while we'll need to keep on using money.

We should be very clear, though, that wealth is independent of the profit system. The more-with-less principle applies whether you're out to "make money" or not. For example, suppose you are an investor and also a philanthropist. With your left hand you invest in a startup. Naturally you expect your "seeds" to become more and more prolific. With your right hand you give to a non-profit cause. If this ends up being money that's "gone" once expended, will you be happy? You shouldn't be. Non-profit seeds are best planted when they too result in a more-with-less harvest. Non-profit dollars, like profit-sector ones, should ideally multiply in ongoing cycles of betterment.

In the years ahead, the distinction between investment and philanthropy or between business and public service may become fuzzy, and that's good. The overall objective is producing more and more true wealth: successive waves of increasing good.

TAKING STEP 2

If you want to create wealth today and you're clear about what true wealth is, the next step is to find a need, problem, or opportunity -- a gap between how things are and how they should be. Below are a few problem-opportunity areas. The supply is endless; there are as many as there are chasms between what people need and what they have.

Need/opportunity 1: Millions of Americans are displaced or disadvantaged by loss of income from farming, manufacturing, and white-collar work. Jobs are being eliminated by technology, or are going overseas through the agency of technology. The ramifications include dying or decaying communities and cities; and closings of local businesses, schools, and other institutions. How might you create wealth (for yourself and others) in this situation? (See the suggestions connected with the seven elements of metamind, below.)

Need/opportunity 2: Americans are caught in a trap of low prices and high real costs. They've been conditioned to shop at big chain stores. They save a few dollars, but the real costs include automotive expense and time to drive to the distant center, destruction of nearby shopping alternatives (stores go out of business when a big chain moves in), low wages for employees, and community degradation with negative impact on real estate values in thousands of towns and suburbs. How might you create wealth in this circumstance? (See the seven-element suggestions below.)

Need/opportunity 3: Reaching companies and government agencies by telephone has become an exercise in frustration. Callers are subjected to long, complex, confusing menus, and wait times that extend into many minutes. And real people -- if they ever materialize -- are not always very helpful. How might you create wealth in this circumstance?

Need/opportunity 4: Farming in third-world countries is too labor-intensive, and the people can't afford megatech tractors, combines, and processing plants. How might you create wealth here?

Need/opportunity 5: America trails other nations in deploying fiber to the home and office for ultra-high-speed communications. How might you create wealth in this situation?

Need/opportunity 6: According to the Census Bureau, in 2002 34.6 million Americans lived below the poverty line, 12.1% of us. The number is up from 32.9 million in 2001. The picture is worse for children under 18, up to 16.7% in 2002 from 16.3% in 2001. How might you create wealth here?

Need/opportunity 7: Advertising has gotten out of hand. Nobody likes the constant bombardment, but broadcasters, publishers, manufacturers, and retailers seem to see no other way to move the goods. How might you create wealth here?

Need/opportunity 8: Big publishers of books, music, and visual art want blockbusters and have all but stopped producing works that promise only small sales. The result is that new, unproven creators have trouble finding an audience; and the public misses out on fresh new ideas and media. How might you create wealth in this circumstance?

Need/opportunity 9: Young people looking for mind-changing escapes find few options other than drugs and alcohol. How might you create wealth here, in a positive way, of course?

Need/opportunity 10: A large part of middle-class income is lost in "friction" such as interest on home mortgages, car loans, and credit-card balances. Late-payment penalties drain off more already-squeezed income. How might you create wealth here?

Wealth-generating problem-opportunities abound, some of them broad (like those above), some more narrow. For example:

- **Millions of Americans, especially older ones, don't know how to maintain the software on their computers and don't want to learn.**

- **In many communities parents drive their kids to school even if the building is only three or four minutes away by foot. The reasons include habit, safety concerns, and guilt at not spending enough time together.**

- **Litter accumulates in public places in spite of full-time custodial staffs.**

- **Everyone seems to need a personal timepiece in order to know what time it is.**

- **Thanks to the varying demands of work, fashion, special events, and the weather, people seem to need or want very large, expensive wardrobes and large spaces in which to store them.**

- **Thanks to burgeoning possessions, it's difficult and expensive to change one's place of residence.**

- **Medical and other insurance often seems not worth the expense, given the lack of complete compensation, high co-payments, and the trouble to make and support claims.**

- **Consumers and business people lack effective control over the rising cost of gasoline, electricity, gas, and other energy sources.**

- **Obesity has become an epidemic in the United States.**

- **Thousands of low-profile facilities are tempting targets to terrorists. They include chemical plants, oil refineries, water reservoirs, and shipping docks.**

- **Millions of people are on track to suffering and dying of AIDS, emphysema, Alzheimer's disease and other ailments.**

How might you create wealth in problem-opportunity areas like these? (See the seven-element suggestions in step 3, below.)

TAKING STEP 3

In every era, there's a hot way to create wealth. In the 1967 movie *The Graduate* starring Dustin Hoffman, a successful businessman whispered into the young man's ear: "plastics." That was the hot thing to focus on then, the road to riches du jour. Earlier in America the mantra was, "Go West, young man!" Gold and a brave new life lay "out there."

What is the hot thing today? Biotech research? Nanotechnology? Health care?

Sure. High tech and essential services are hot and will get hotter. The very hottest thing, in my view, is something else, something more basic and human: consciousness.

The golden path to enormous wealth in the 21st century is to utilize and enhance metamind. Many examples support this claim. First I'll illustrate the wealth-creating potential of intentional consciousness in general, and then show how each of the seven elements of metamind can trigger billions in value for smart business people and their customers. Finally, I'll illustrate the hyper-wealth-generating potential of electronic systems in tandem with metamind when metamind calls the shots.

Wealth Through Metamind in General

Money flows where metamind is because metamind is what people want. They thrive on it and get depressed or mad without it. If you're in retail sales or offer a service, metamind is your gold mine. Wealth producing effects kicks in when you "fill your space with consciousness."

Think of a Disney theme park. Why does it work? Why do people want to be there and gladly plunk their money down? The attractions, of course: the rides, the thrills and aha's, the beautiful environment, the food. However, behind it all there's a magic ingredient: the thousands of Disney "cast members" (that's what all guest-facing employees are called) who project their consciousness into every nook and cranny of the place.

A candy wrapper misses a trashcan, or an ice cream cone plops to the ground. It doesn't stay there long. An alert cast member picks it up or sees that it's cleaned up. Pronto. Vigilance is acute and intentional. No inch of a Disney park lacks the warm radiance of awareness. Disney cast members are selected for their social skills and positive personalities, among other things.

A child is crying? Hey, that won't do. A cast member notices and goes into cheer-up mode. A line is too long and people seem edgy? Hey, that won't do. Figure out a way to make lines shorter, or add entertainments that make waiting in line an event in itself.

People gravitate to a human presence. A study was done on the use of park benches. The most popular benches, it turned out, were not those facing beautiful natural vistas such as lakes. People preferred the benches that faced human vistas: people walking, talking, or playing games. The human mind homes in on spaces filled with the common consciousness of others.

Where there is consciousness, especially intentional consciousness or metamind, people not only aggregate but also spend money. Many of our train stations have lost their human attendants and have become inhospitable as a result. This is one reason the railroads are in trouble.

Awhile back my wife and I were planning to go to the theater in New York City, from our home in northern New Jersey. I considered traveling by train instead of car. It might be less hassle, I thought, and the cost was about the same.

But the condition of the station gave me pause. There were two sets of tracks with a boarded-up station house at the edge of one and an open-air shelter at the edge of the other. It was unclear where we should stand and there was no one to ask. The place had a barren feel. No nicely tended shrubs or flowers, just weeds. Rust and obsolescence all around. Nobody selling nice hot coffee or magazines.

No life to the place. No consciousness. So we went to New York by car as usual. The railroad lost our fares and moved a few seconds closer to bankruptcy.

Contrast this railroad to a Disney-run conveyance. Whether old-fashioned trolley or monorail, you can be sure it would be surrounded by consciousness. Everything would be clean and polished and attended, made welcoming by "cast members" exuding an omnipresent cocoon of never-flagging attentiveness and spirit. Disney and other purveyors of consciousness will get our fares.

An infusion of consciousness will help you build wealth whether you run a restaurant, gas station, insurance agency, construction business, software development shop, research lab, airline, or international bank. It's vital beyond the customer interface. Once it's lost among employees, rapport and morale start to fade, innovation wanes, problems get overlooked, solutions take longer to implement, and mistakes aggregate.

On the other hand, if you boost the level of consciousness among all your people, spirits brighten, ideas bubble up, problems are foreseen before they happen, and fixes get made more rapidly.

Wealth for a company comes ultimately from employees working together effectively. A winning group is in fact a "company" in an original sense of the word. It's a close-knit assemblage that has developed synergy over time. That synergy is experienced as group consciousness consisting of individual and shared enthusiasm, warmth, ideation, decision, action, discovery, social interaction, and responsibility. It's a magical thing; and if you mess with it, you damage your wealth-building engine.

There are many ways to wreck your wealth engine. For example, micromanagement, withdrawing responsibility, and inciting competition and contention where cooperation belongs. The surest way to degrade the engine is to get rid of some of the group's members or to scatter them in ways that make them start from scratch in building a new engine.

Before the breakup of AT&T, Bell Labs was a wealth-building engine that hummed with electric synergy and glowed with common consciousness. At the Holmdel facility, for example, employees planted vegetable gardens and went on hikes together. Bell

Labs people started a symphony orchestra in their spare time. Ideas leaped from mind to mind in delightful interplay, giving us discoveries such as the first evidence of the big bang that launched the universe, and inventions such as the transistor, which launched the electronics revolution.

Then, with the government-mandated deregulation of telecommunications, Bell Labs was broken up. Some of the people were shunted to a new company, Lucent Technologies. The rest stayed with AT&T as AT&T Labs. With the breakup the magical common consciousness got broken too. Subsequent reorganizations and downsizings did not help. Lucent's stock is hovering well below $4, down from a high of $65. At AT&T Labs, morale is well off its high and there are rumors that the operation might be sold or disbanded.

Wealth materializes where metamind is. But there is more to the magic of metamind than its general glow. The rainbow hues of its seven components also point to pots of gold.

Wealth Through Basic
Thinking Skills & Symbolism

Basic thinking skills, the atoms of metamind, deal with elements such as color, shape, size, order ... class, structure, operation ... and analogical similarity. These elements support (usually below the veil of awareness) the macro entities of discovery, creativity, decision making, and responsibility.

Symbolism is the conveyor belt of these elemental, basic functions as well as of the macro ones. Symbolic entities relevant to business are of course words, logos, and corporate images.

Sometimes intentionally calling upon the elemental processes can be extremely productive. It can make the difference between success and failure, and produce great wealth. Consider a brand that is about to expand into the American market: Juan Valdez coffee, to be sold in retail outlets in competition with Starbucks.

Consumer mind space is limited, so it's important to get a buying message across economically, quickly, and effectively. The right image (name and logo) can achieve this. How might symbolism and the basic skills apply to introducing the Juan Valdez brand effectively? And how might the elements of thought figure in an effective response by Starbucks?

First, it's fortunate for the Colombian organization that the Juan Valdez name and logo already exist and have a place in consumer awareness. You can probably bring the Juan Valdez logo to mind (it's Juan's face with a donkey and a mountain in the background). Quick, what's the Starbucks logo? Many people can't say. (It's a circle with crowned princess in the middle.)

So, the National Federation of Coffee Growers of Columbia (the organization behind Juan Valdez) may have a more visually impressive logo than Starbucks. But companies are symbolized by ear as well as eye. "Starbucks" rolls easily off the tongue and is only two syllables. "Juan Valdez" is three syllables and perhaps less effective out loud.

Should Starbucks consider developing a more memorable visual logo, and should the Columbians consider a shorter name, such as "Valdez" only or "Juan" only?

"I'll meet you at Starbucks."
"I'll meet you at Juan's."
Both names roll easily off the tongue.

Such questions are worthy of thought and study since millions of dollars ride on the consumer response. If changes are indicated, then the elemental skills might be called upon intentionally to develop creative variations (alternative colors, shapes and designs, sizes, metaphorical associations, and so on). Of course the managements behind the Starbucks and Juan Valdez brands will be smart if they cultivate high levels of consciousness among their idea people. The best solutions emerge in an atmosphere of free-reigning creativity, positive spirit, and fun (the top metamind atmosphere described in chapter 6).

Wealth Through Conscious Monitoring & Control

A friend of mine in upstate New York was cutting small logs with a chain saw. For two hours the fireplace-sized pieces flew off the whirring blade into a pile. He had hit a nice rhythm, but his mind must have wandered. "Yeaowww!" Blood flowed from his left hand. The cause? A momentary loss of attention. (The wound was stitched and all turned out well.)

Accidents have many causes. The chief one: lack of consciousness. Attention can lapse for only an instant, and zap, you're toast. Auto accidents, industrial accidents, and accidents in the home -- they all tend to happen when awareness fades. I used to spend a fair amount of time in print shops. One of the gadgets that intrigued me was the large industrial-strength paper cutter. The wide, razor-sharp blade could cut through a stack of sheets a foot high as if it were butter. All sorts of safety measures had been built in, but printers told me people still somehow managed to get shirtsleeves or fingers into harms way. The cause was always the same. Momentary inattention; not thinking, not seeing.

Accidents cost businesses billions a year in avoidable medical costs, insurance, and lost productivity. Conscious monitoring and control is the metamind skill that prevents accidents, but it's good for much more. It also prevents costly mistakes and missed opportunities.

To err is human, but catching errors before they happen is a better way to be human. That takes alertness, attention, concern, and awareness -- in a word, consciousness. Packages get sent to the wrong address, the wrong size or quantity is ordered, deadlines or promises are forgotten. Such lapses, all due to degraded monitoring and control, cost uncounted billions. Through reduction of their number, enormous sums can be added to corporate bottom lines.

Missing opportunities can be just as costly as missing problems, perhaps even more so. Seeing opportunities requires the same sharpness of awareness. A sports fan I know kicked himself because he was too preoccupied to notice a free parking space near Giants Stadium in New York. He saw it a couple of seconds too late as a more alert driver moved in. No other on-street space was to be found, and it took him 45 minutes to park in a public garage and make it to the stadium. A small thing, but illustrative of mental lapses that needlessly siphon off billions in profits.

The people at General Electric Capital Aviation Services normally do a crack job of monitoring industry trends for new moneymaking possibilities. Somehow, though, they failed to perceive what competitive companies saw back in 2000: a market for buying and leasing 50-passenger regional jets. "We missed that opportunity," said President Henry Hubschman. "We realize that was a mistake and we're not about to miss that opportunity again." After losing considerable business, GECAS got into the game with a $12 billion purchase of regional jets.

Mental acuteness and knowledge are vital components in the opportunity-seeking aspect of the monitoring process. On them ride billions of dollars plus or minus.

The other forward-looking aspect of monitoring is potential problem detection. Accident-prone drivers fail to focus on potential negatives; safe drivers keep mindful of possible dangers on every side and visualize in advance how to react. NASA engineers excel at monitoring systems for any faint possibility of future trouble. Yet even they sometimes fail to fathom everything. On Jan. 28, 1986, the shuttle *Challenger* exploded sixty seconds after launch because of the failure of an O-ring, a faulty component that allowed fuel to leak and ignite. The disaster killed seven astronauts and caused more than a two-year delay in shuttle launchings.

If you want to create wealth through conscious monitoring and control, you'll build this skill in yourself and your colleagues. How? Reminders and mental models can help. For example, master carpenters advise their apprentices, "Measure twice and cut once."

No metamental skill, however, can be fully developed all on its own. You've got to make everything better in order to make any one thing really good. For example, it's hard to be fully alert if you're sleepy. If employees are drowsy because they're eating wrong, or not getting enough exercise or sleep, your opportunity may be to help them improve their lifestyles. If drugs or personal problems make them mentally vacant, your opportunity is to do whatever it takes to help restore their mental focus.

One solution to faulty human awareness is to replace people with electronic monitoring alternatives. However, as pointed out elsewhere in this book, the path of human replacement leads to the overall failure of the planet. The best option is to build better monitoring systems while simultaneously enhancing human monitoring skills in a society where everyone has a place.

Wealth Through Hypothesizing

Several years ago a client of mine, a large multinational corporation, had a problem. A large manufacturing plant they were building in Europe developed cracks in its concrete columns. The foundation was in, the concrete floor had been poured, and the roof was up, but no work had been started on the walls. Construction was halted pending an investigation of the cracking.

Was there a problem with the concrete mixture? Did the columns need to be knocked down and replaced with new columns made of better stuff? A construction consultant suspected foundation settlement and recommended a site study.

The situation looked bad. If the concrete mixture was the cause of the cracking, hundreds of thousands of dollars would be required to re-do the columns and roof, and thousands of dollars more would be lost for each day construction was extended, since production of saleable products could not begin. If settlement was the cause and the site was susceptible to further settlement, maybe the site would have to be abandoned. In this case, millions of dollars would be lost.

The situation seemed to call for immediate decision making. Authorize the site study, check out the concrete mixture, or both. That, it seemed, would be the intelligent thing to do, the path of advanced executive consciousness. However, metamind -- our wealth builder -- does not always perform as one might expect.

The way to invoke metamind at its best is to make yourself and colleagues more human in all ways. Get

243

into a positive frame of mind, atmosphere 1 (described in chapter 6). Lighten up, brighten up, laugh, look, get curious, question, see, focus ... and call up your best mental models, such as, "let's not jump to cause."

When company representatives on the site started looking at the columns without mental stress, glazed eyes, and preconceptions, they noticed something interesting. The cracks were only vertical, not horizontal, and only at the very tops of the columns, never at the bottom or in the middle. If there was something wrong with the concrete mixture, or if the foundation had settled, wouldn't there be cracks all over the place?

There must be a third possible cause, and there was. It turned out to be roof expansion. Sun on the roof had caused the roof area to grow in all directions, forcing the columns outward and generating the cracks. A relatively simple solution, addition of better expansion joints, was implemented.

Discovery is an alert, alive activity that is rather like child's play. It's fun. It's engrossing. You get to play Sherlock Holmes, sleuthing and finding things out ... perceiving, seeing, exploring ... wondering and learning. Discovery is at the root of all fixes in business, all scientific knowledge, and all engineering improvements. The vast industrial wealth generated over the past few centuries has its roots in discovery.

Wealth Through
Creativity & Imagination

From the perspective of higher consciousness, opportunities abound. The world is filled with problems, distressing situations, and difficulties of all types. To the creative mind, these negative situations are seen as golden. They all get converted into opportunities.

Consider problem/opportunity 1, above: "Millions of Americans are displaced or disadvantaged by loss of income from farming, manufacturing, and white-collar work." What might metamind do with this situation through its creative channel? Think of the three displaced groups: farmers, manufacturing employees, and white-collar personnel including many high-tech people. Then let your imagination roam.

What synergies might the three groups have if combined in local environments? Put on your real estate, architecture, engineering, or business development hat. There are whole towns that you could almost buy for a song, many wired with fiber. Think of the intercommunity concept described in chapter 7. What could you create in the right small town in the right place, or in part of depressed Philadelphia, Chicago, or Jamestown?

Think of the skills of the three displaced groups. How might these skills be activated in new ways? Remember, just about anything is fair game for the creative metamind. For example, urban agriculture and local food processing merging with "free" construction in the style of Habitat-for-Humanity. Or the integration of these elements with local artistic creation, inexpensive higher education, and new high-tech services offered over the information superhighway.

Consider problem/opportunity 2, above: "Americans are caught in a trap of low prices and high real costs." Let your imagination loose. Put on your retail sales, merchandising, and advertising hats. What new distribution model might you invent? What process might offer more real value than a big chain store, without the high hidden costs?

How could you set it up and communicate it? Your plan might involve establishing a new national operation, or bolstering a small retail business that is threatened. For example, what are several alternative ways to set up a retail distribution system? Something involving network marketing, maybe, or local co-ops? Or how about an association of small retailers banding together in a larger presence, like the association of Columbian coffee bean growers who are going to compete with Starbucks under their Juan Valdez image?

Does your distribution system have to be based on buildings that people have to go to? How about a mobile solution? What about a consumer-owned or supplier-owned entity?

Consider problem/opportunity 3, above: "Reaching companies and government agencies by telephone has become an exercise in frustration." What's the wealth-creating opportunity here? If you run a small or large company, how might you set up your phone system differently? Suppose you delighted people with your system rather than taking their time and making them mad; you might enjoy significantly increased sales and customer loyalty.

The GE Answer Center used to pride itself on rewarding the caller with a real person by the third ring; and that person could answer any question on any GE product from a light bulb to a jet engine, thanks to a computer system that the representative accessed. Today GE's answer center has degenerated to a system like "everyone else's" that assaults callers with multiple menus, ads, and standard excuses, "due to high caller volume, the wait time is ..."

Perhaps you could dream up a customer-friendly system that would be more like GE's old system, and really make your business fly. Or maybe there's a new service you could create, one that employs people to handle calls for corporate customers cost-effectively yet with regard to the value of the caller's time.

Reflect that the federal don't-call list prevents tele-marketers from making outgoing sales calls. How could you turn this to advantage? Perhaps you could create a human experience so compelling that lots of people will want to call *you*.

Every year billions of dollars of sales are made by phone or followed up by phone. You could have a piece of it by making life easier for millions of frustrated Americans.

Creativity and imagination create wealth because they create options for more with less -- new things of increasing value that people will gladly pay money for.

247

How can you mine more creativity in yourself and others? Anything you can do to enhance overall consciousness -- with its glow of delight, connection, and fun -- will foster creativity.

Specific methods include withholding judgment until you reach the decision making stage, and intentionally invoking the basic thinking skills (qualification, structure analysis and so on) to generate new combinations and variations.

For Hoffmann LaRoche a few years ago, I developed "The Bright Idea Program." The aim was to help improve operations through creative thinking and suggestions for change. Everyone was invited to reconsider the size, shape, order and other qualities of products, business operations, and manufacturing processes. The result was over $3 million per year in savings plus a boost in employee empowerment.

The wealth-triggering power of creativity may be applied to --

- Improving an existing business.
- Coming up with a new business venture or product.
- Attacking causes of problems identified in the hypothesis process.
- Eliminating potential problems and risks identified in the monitoring process.

Wealth Through
Subjective Decision Making

Good decisions, stemming from metamind, often create considerable wealth. That's been true for the aggregate decisions of IBM, now bringing the company over $81 billion a year.

Decision making affects reality by instigating one series of events versus another. Go or no go; do X or do nothing; go route A or route B; choose among A, B, C or D. In 1980 IBM executives made a conscious decision to create a personal computer, code named the "Acorn," which would appear in 1981 as the IBM PC. The executives might have consciously decided to stay out of the PC business. If they had, who knows what IBM would be today? Probably a smaller, poorer enterprise.

Decision making has the greatest wealth-creating leverage when it's most conscious and alive. But "conscious" is a tricky word. For example, if you consciously, intentionally make a decision in a boardroom, you may or may not be operating at the highest possible level of metamind. "We need to decide between X and Y. Let's start by reviewing our objectives ..."

Your very deliberate boardroom decision might be excellent, but the most powerful, future-shaping decisions tend to be made less formally, much faster and on the go, almost casually sometimes, and in a spirit of flow and enthusiasm. Such decisions rank high on the subjective scale, too, though often involving much critical analysis.

IBM created billions of dollars of wealth through its PC decision, but that decision played second fiddle to an earlier one. The primary decision -- the one that triggered ALL the billions of the microcomputer era -- was made by two young Californians working on their own, Steve Wozniak and Steve Jobs. They never formally "decided" to create the world's first personal computer. "Shall we invent the microcomputer or not?" Rather, they enjoyed a high level of metamind and let nature take its course through a series of quick casual decisions followed by actions followed by more quick casual decisions.

They had fun tinkering, inventing, and dreaming. Wozniak was motivated by the science and engineering of computing; Jobs was more turned on by entrepreneurial creativity.

They both belonged to the Homebrew Computer Club founded by Wozniak. At that time, 1974, computers were refrigerator-sized "IBM machines" for companies with deep pockets. Wozniak and Jobs wanted one of the gadgets so they could indulge their fascination with computing. They didn't have the asking price, so they scrounged around for parts and tried to assemble a device of their own.

At that point, they might have made the "decision" just to create their personal plaything and stop there. But Jobs had visions of a possible market. Maybe there were other hobbyists, like them, who would also like a cheap gadget to play around with.

Once the basic decision was made -- to try to create a device that could be sold -- many other decisions followed. Jobs and Wozniak had no money to develop and manufacture the devices, so they looked for alternative ways of raising cash. Approach investors? Get a bank loan? They decided on a third option, scrounging. Wozniak sold his scientific calculator and Jobs sold his Volkswagen microbus for a total of $1,300. Then they talked local electronics suppliers into giving them components on consignment. The result was the Apple I, which brought them sales of $774,000.

About six years after Wozniak and Jobs made their basic decision, the IBM executives made theirs, to develop the IBM PC. Many subsidiary decisions followed. One significant one -- illustrating the value of metamind -- was to locate the development effort in Boca Raton, Florida, rather than in New York at one of IBM's prestigious development labs. William Lowe, who headed the effort, felt that his twelve engineers could work better in a creative atmosphere free of corporate bureaucracy. The group quickly bonded in a blur of enthusiasm that yielded the powerful, affordable device that was released on August 12, 1981. It was the first non-human to be named "man of the year" by Time Magazine, in 1982.

Wealth Through Social skills

There are two farmers' markets near our home. Both offer excellent produce and both seem to have been doing equally well until recently. Then, a few months ago, one of them started to take off. More people started going there, buying grew more brisk, and the items offered grew in number. How come?

Both are family-owned businesses and both hire employees to help out. Until recently, both seemed to have the attitude, "You're here to buy our stuff. We're glad to help you, but the stuff is really all you're after." At both establishments the customer would walk past the bins, pick out a few apples or ears of corn, maybe some squash or tomatoes, and plunk their selections down on the counter. A clerk would ring up the total and that was that. Fine.

But one of the establishments started operating a little differently. Customers entering the establishment were greeted with, "Hello." Eye contact was made. There was a smile. If a customer wanted to ask about a variety of apple or potato, or talk about the weather, advice or friendly conversation was readily available. It was hard to distinguish between an owner and an employee because everyone there displayed excellent social skills.

Social skills make a huge difference in business. They depend primarily on consciousness -- noticing, for starters, that somebody is there. In restaurants, stores, and offices, there are few things as annoying as being ignored; and few things as refreshing as being not only seen but also seen within a positive, friendly, helpful aura of awareness.

Social skills generate wealth like crazy. For every dollar you spend helping your associates become more outgoing and inclusive, you'll get back many dollars in return. The socially conscious farmers' market has constructed a larger building and added new products such as craft items and wrought-iron garden decorations. They've added attractions for families with kids: a petting zoo, a hay-bale maze, and a large wooden train. They've even added a restroom for people who want to hang out for extended periods. Their former vegetable stand is starting to look like a theme park.

Wealth Through Responsibility

A great way to increase wealth is to increase responsibility in associates and yourself. Suppose you run a magazine or newspaper and employ a woman who sells advertising space. Her job is to attract advertisers and take their orders.

One day a customer asks her for help with the copy and layout of an ad. If you've defined her job narrowly and she's overworked, she probably won't offer any help. It's not part of her job. However, if you've empowered her to take responsibility and view the business from your broad perspective, she may think, "I want to make this customer happy. We need all the business we can get. I'm really busy, but sure, I'll give him a hand." The second, broader perspective will build your business faster than almost anything else.

In the late 1800's a young space salesman was asked by a customer for some help with ad copy and layout. He said yes. Other customers began asking for his help too, and he gave it gladly. Eventually, when the requests reached a critical volume, the young man decided to turn his helpfulness into a new business service. His name was J. Walter Thompson, and he set up the world's first advertising agency -- the J. Walter Thompson Company, which now takes in almost a billion dollars a year.

If you want to create wealth through responsibility, remember that it is something that is both given and assumed. It's smart to surround yourself with people who just naturally have a sense of responsibility and want to assume more. And it's smart to enhance their responsibility as much as you can.

Responsibility is the wide exercise of consciousness that takes in, ultimately, the whole planet. It encompasses and directs perception as well as caring, intention, values, and action. Its aim is to do well within the scope of its compass. A feeling of ownership or stewardship extends to the limits of its defined breadth. An associate's sense of responsibility can extend to the limits of a desk, department, company, company including its customers, or beyond. That depends in roughly equal parts on the associate and you.

Today as always, responsibility is the yellow brick road to more and more of everything good. You can, of course, get filthy rich without it -- if your game is diverting money in the process of destroying wealth.

Wealth Through
Metamind plus Megatech

I've given examples of creating wealth through higher consciousness and accentuation of the human factor. Wealth (not just money cornering) can also be created by *eliminating* human functions in creative ways, so long as it's not part of a general trend toward middle-class genocide.

Many supermarkets are setting up self-service checkout stations as an alternative to higher-cost human checkers. One result of this trend could be the creation of sterile, vacant markets where unemployed people -- like the former checkers, gas station attendants, factory workers, and infotech specialists -- come to spend their pennies in lonesome isolation. Another result of the trend could be the conversion of the checkers into food specialists who monitor the store, offer advice, discuss recipes, and so on.

If this idea seems outlandish, consider that Costco already does something like it. They hire people to prepare and hand out food samples. The attendants don't do it robotically. They say "hi" and answer questions.

> **NOTE:** Many customers say they prefer automated systems to live checkers and attendants. Greater efficiency is one reason they give, and they have a point. Another reason is that they find the human interaction a bit stressful and unpleasant, and they have a point here too. Many customer-facing

personnel have withdrawn their consciousness. They no longer bother to look at the customer, be friendly, or say more than the absolute minimum. When employees act like robots, they might as well be robots.

Heightening consciousness and going electronic are not at all mutually exclusive. In fact they can work together beautifully. Combining the two trends synergistically can lead to vast new wealth and a future we'll all like very much. Costco is highly efficient and automated, yet they fill their superstores with more than minimal consciousness. Home Depot also fills their space with technological efficiency as well as human consciousness through advice on projects.

A Disney theme park is perhaps the most graphic example of high-tech efficiency combined with the glow of human awareness. Automated conveyances, futuristic attractions, and electronic security systems work in harmony with visitors embraced by helpful, positive cast members on every side.

I believe the ideal future for us is neither an ultra-robotic one devoid of the human factor, nor a human one that makes people keep on performing mindless, robotic functions such as scanning groceries, pumping gas, answering simple questions on the phone, slaughtering cattle, or assembling widgets. In our best tomorrow, consciousness and technology will advance in tandem, with consciousness in charge.

A CASE HISTORY

Suppose you've just become president of Nadir Bank, a rural chain with four branches. Nadir has stayed about the same for over forty years. No growth.

The chairman of the board fears that a puny future will be the bank's fate, but wishes it could be otherwise. What would you do?

a. **Cut people to make the operation leaner and more profitable.**
b. **Tell everyone to brighten their consciousness.**
c. **Introduce a new line of business, Nadir Coffee.**

Option "a" might add to the bottom line temporarily, but is it worth the assault on employee consciousness? Might it backfire and start the bank on a downhill path? The "school book" answer, "b," would probably be ineffectual, even silly, in practice -- rather like telling everyone to improve their attitude. Option "c" is of course ridiculous.

So, what would you really do? What's a good, practical way to increase wealth in this situation?

In 1993 Raymond Davis took over as president of Umpqua Bank, Portland, Oregon. It had just four branches. It had experienced no growth over the past 40 years and its prospects seemed minimal.

Davis developed a radical strategy for building up the operation. It was to focus on culture as "our most

257

valuable asset," a concept that would embrace employees, customers, and the surrounding communities. In essence, Davis went with option "b," above, except he did more than talk. He developed very tangible action elements.

Breaking with standard banking roles such as teller, he implemented the concept of the Universal Associate. Each Associate was authorized to help customers with any need related to anything the bank did. Every employee was to be a salesperson, customer care agent, loan officer, and so forth. Davis introduced sales training like that offered at Nordstrom's. Given such empowerment, people gained a sense of ownership and blossomed with newfound dedication and initiative.

Davis created a new culture for customers, too. A bank didn't have to be a sterile place where people came simply to put money in or take it out. A bank could be a nice place to be, a hangout where people could linger and do a variety of things. Davis started calling his branches "stores" and outfitted them with computer café's, postal centers, wide-screen financial news broadcasts, and terminals for surfing the Internet.

The new décor included plush leather chairs and coffee tables. There were also displays of logo merchandise featuring the Umpqua brand. And, oh yes, Davis introduced a special blend of Umpqua-branded coffee. Customers could drink it on the premises in Umpqua mugs or buy some to brew at home.

Davis introduced electronic innovations along with the human ones. Special software now measures the service level branch by branch. Feedback helps employees improve and singles out excellent behaviors for emulation.

In just ten years, Umpqua has grown from four branches to 64, the largest community bank in Oregon. It has over 1,000 employees, $2.6 billion in assets, and a subsidiary that offers brokerage services. Davis plans to expand as far north as Seattle and as far south as Sacramento. He now has an Executive Vice President of Culture to help ensure that his winning strategy remains in force.

11

What You Can Do Now

Personal Steps for a Better Future

Business, government, and our whole society need to change if we're to survive the brain-drain trend, get beyond technogreed, and create the fully alive, human world we all want. But as individuals we don't need to wait. Here are nine things each of us can start doing right now:

1. **Gradually move to work high on the hyper-human scale.** In the near term, there will be money in the old know-how occupations for many. Longer-term, smart, zippy systems will prevail. If a form of work takes creativity, goal-focus, ethical behavior, responsibility, and social skills, it's likely to have a future and

260

generate income eventually if not right away. Entrepreneurship will be in demand for a long time, as will intrapreneurship within companies. So will scientific research requiring "aha's," health care, education, and social services of all types. If an endeavor requires vision and caring, if there's a need for it and you love it, it just might be the thing that makes you money at some point.

2. **Constantly hone your hyper-human skills.** Be a generalist and get better at everything that makes people special, from caring to creating to persuasion. That will help your bottom line in any work at any time. Regain control over your cultural life: TV, newspapers, the Internet, and other media. Observe the mind manipulation that's ever-present, and get above it.

3. **Transform your job or situation by applying the seven phases of metamind.** You can increase your wealth and advance toward your goals by developing analogs of the examples in chapter 10.

4. **Cut back.** Don't count on corporate or social policy to protect your livelihood. In the absence of reform, you may need to compete with an Indian or Chinese pro willing to work for a few thousand dollars a year. Assume that U.S. employers will use the pressure of foreign pay

scales to negotiate lower pay domestically. All exportable jobs will gravitate toward a world pay scale; and it will be lower than current U.S. rates. Find ways to live better on less. For example, can you get along with just one car, or none?

5. **Start adjusting your lifestyle to "inter-community" mode.** (See chapter 7.) Walk more, drive less. Avail yourself of, or create, local cultural activities rather than always driving to far-away mass events. Do some local food production, if only growing tomatoes or mung sprouts. Develop at-home or walking-distance ways of earning money. Make in-creasing, practical use of the Internet, especially broadband services.

6. **Develop meta-conscious ways of doing every-thing:** listening to music, watching a movie, experiencing ads, conducting casual conversa-tions, walking down the street, eating, sleeping, interacting with store clerks, and influencing the actions of others.... From time to time, ask yourself what you're doing, and then watch yourself do it. This approach, used in all meditation, automatically pops you up into metamind, conveying greater appreciation and self-mastery.

7. **Fill physical spaces with your consciousness.** Be acutely aware and mindful in your home, the workplace, stores, meeting places, parks, and playing fields. Take responsibility for all these places, their cleanliness and beauty, their safety, and the mood and activities of people present.

8. **Be active politically.** It's our own fault if "they" eat our lunch. Have an impact on the quality of your community, occupational field, geographic region, nation, and world.

9. **Join with other people in promoting hyper-human development.** See www.eranova.com for opportunities.

The winning strategy for the information age is to inject "aliveness," including deliberate reflection and re-sponsibility, into everything we do, and let electronic systems take over the routine tasks.

Let's go with the brain-drain flow, tame megatech with its technogreed bias, and come out on top. With clear perception and the right actions, we can avoid chaos and surf today's trend to the future we want.

In this book I've often addressed my remarks to leaders in business, government, technical development, edu-cation, the arts and sciences, religion and social work. If you're among them, you're on the starting lineup for reaching the goal we all want. If you do not consider youself a leader -- maybe you're unemployed or have a low-paid job in a store, office, shop, or the military -- I speak to you too. The name of leader belongs to anyone who does the right thing first, regardless of position.

I also speak to young people in college and high school. If you're among them, your spirit and contributions may be the most important of all. How you think and feel, what you are, and how you act will go far beyond the forward charge of today's starting lineup; and there are things you can do immediately to move us forward.

I feel that the message of this book isn't quite complete. A good case has been made, I believe, for overcoming human negatives including technogreed ... for developing technology to serve people rather than replace them ... for heightening our metamind skills of basic thinking, monitoring, discovery, creativity, decision making, social interaction, and responsibility ... for brightening our overall aliveness ... and for changing our political, business, and social institutions with bold intelligence and courage.

Something is missing, though: the tying of a small knot to bring everything together. Young people are in my mind as I try to tie that knot. My final words are for them, but include everyone who is young at heart.

Consider that the "I" that I now use is the priviliged "I" of all authors, whose voices endure, however undeserved, through the magic of publishing for as long as there are readers who come across their words. Consider that the "I" that I now use is the "I" of a larger voice, not mine.

What do I expect of you? What do I want from you? You're an alive being in charge of your own aliveness and responsible for the aliveness of everyone on the planet, now and future.

Of course I want you to master the complex task of marshalling, monitoring, and managing all your human qualities along lines unique to you that serve the evolving general good. But I want more than that of you. I want what I believe you want for yourself: something spectacular and transcendent.

I don't want you to merely meet my expectations; I want you to ignite my surprise. I don't want you to merely win my respect; I want you to command my admiration. I don't want you to merely cause me to like you; through your actions and your being I want you to *make* me -- beyond all preconception or distraction -- love you.

Other Resources

Additional information, updates, action options, and links are available at **www.eranova.com**.